# The Assassination of John F. Kennedy

Carolyn McAuliffe, *Book Editor*

Daniel Leone, *President*
Bonnie Szumski, *Publisher*
Scott Barbour, *Managing Editor*

**AT ISSUE IN HISTORY**

GREENHAVEN
PRESS®

San Diego • Detroit • New York • San Francisco • Cleveland
New Haven, Conn. • Waterville, Maine • London • Munich

© 2003 by Greenhaven Press. Greenhaven Press is an imprint of The Gale Group, Inc., a division of Thomson Learning, Inc.

Greenhaven® and Thomson Learning™ are trademarks used herein under license.

*For more information, contact*
Greenhaven Press
27500 Drake Rd.
Farmington Hills, MI 48331-3535
Or you can visit our Internet site at http://www.gale.com

Cover credit: © Hulton/Archive by Getty Images

John F. Kennedy Library, 10

**LIBRARY OF CONGRESS CATALOGING-IN-PUBLICATION DATA**

The assassination of John F. Kennedy / Carolyn McAuliffe, book editor.
    p. cm. — (At issue in history)
Includes bibliographical references and index.
ISBN 0-7377-1355-0 (pbk. : alk. paper) — ISBN 0-7377-1354-2 (lib. : alk. paper)
    1. Kennedy, John F. (John Fitzgerald), 1917–1963—Assassination. 2. Kennedy, John F. (John Fitzgerald), 1917–1936—Assassination—Sources. I. Title: Assassination of John F. Kennedy. II. McAuliffe, Carolyn. III. Series.
E842.9 .A775 2003
364.15'24'097309046—dc21
                                                2002035391

Printed in the United States of America

# Contents

mony of eyewitnesses. That testimony, a misidentified murder weapon, and a "magic bullet" that somehow struck both the president and the Texas governor—added up to a confused mountain of evidence and caused many to discredit the commission's final report.

# Chapter 2: The Conspiracy Theories

ernment officials had Kennedy killed in order to prevent him from implementing his plan to remove U.S. soldiers from Vietnam.

# Foreword

Historian Robert Weiss defines history simply as "a record and interpretation of past events." Both elements—record and interpretation—are necessary, Weiss argues.

> Names, dates, places, and events are the essence of history. But historical writing is not a compendium of facts. It consists of facts placed in a sequence to tell a connected story. A work of history is not merely a story, however. It also must analyze what happened and *why*—that is, it must interpret the past for the reader.

For example, the events of December 7, 1941, that led President Franklin D. Roosevelt to call it "a date which will live in infamy" are fairly well known and straightforward. A force of Japanese planes and submarines launched a torpedo and bombing attack on American military targets in Pearl Harbor, Hawaii. The surprise assault sank five battleships, disabled or sank fourteen additional ships, and left almost twenty-four hundred American soldiers and sailors dead. On the following day, the United States formally entered World War II when Congress declared war on Japan.

These facts and consequences were almost immediately communicated to the American people who heard reports about Pearl Harbor and President Roosevelt's response on the radio. All realized that this was an important and pivotal event in American and world history. Yet the news from Pearl Harbor raised many unanswered questions. Why did Japan decide to launch such an offensive? Why were the attackers so successful in catching America by surprise? What did the attack reveal about the two nations, their people, and their leadership? What were its causes, and what were its effects? Political leaders, academic historians, and students look to learn the basic facts of historical events and to read the intepretations of these events by many different sources, both primary and secondary, in order to develop a more complete picture of the event in a historical context.

In the case of Pearl Harbor, several important questions surrounding the event remain in dispute, most notably the role of President Roosevelt. Some historians have blamed his policies for deliberately provoking Japan to attack in order to propel America into World War II; a few have gone so far as to accuse him of knowing of the impending attack but not informing others. Other historians, examining the same event, have exonerated the president of such charges, arguing that the historical evidence does not support such a theory.

The Greenhaven At Issue in History series recognizes that many important historical events have been interpreted differently and in some cases remain shrouded in controversy. Each volume features a collection of articles that focus on a topic that has sparked controversy among eyewitnesses, contemporary observers, and historians. An introductory essay sets the stage for each topic by presenting background and context. Several chapters then examine different facets of the subject at hand with readings chosen for their diversity of opinion. Each selection is preceded by a summary of the author's main points and conclusions. A bibliography is included for those students interested in pursuing further research. An annotated table of contents and thorough index help readers to quickly locate material of interest. Taken together, the contents of each of the volumes in the Greenhaven At Issue in History series will help students become more discriminating and thoughtful readers of history.

# Introduction

In his inaugural address on January 20, 1961, President John Fitzgerald Kennedy challenged the nation: "And so, my fellow Americans, ask not what your country can do for you; ask what you can do for your country." At the age of forty-three, John F. Kennedy was the youngest president to ever be elected and the first Roman Catholic to hold that office. Despite his brief term in office—less than three years— many Americans held Kennedy in high esteem due to his enthusiasm and his commitment to improve the quality of life in the nation. Kennedy's untimely death at the hands of assassins was mourned throughout the United States and around the world. The nation's great sense of loss was compounded by questions concerning the assassination, questions that continue to this day.

## The Dallas Motorcade

In November 1963, Kennedy's campaign trail for reelection led him to the state of Texas. On November 22, following a morning speech, Kennedy joined his wife, Jacqueline; John B. Connally Jr., the governor of Texas; and Mrs. Connally in a motorcade through the streets of Dallas. The motorcade was scheduled to culminate in a luncheon at the Trade Mart. Eight Secret Service agents followed the president's limousine in a separate car and scanned the crowds, streets, and buildings for possible signs of trouble.

President Kennedy, Governor Connally, and their wives were greeted with enthusiasm as the presidential limousine made its way through Dallas. The motorcade made several stops so that the president could acknowledge the friendly crowds. The spectators welcomed Kennedy with open arms, proving his enormous popularity. At one point Mrs. Connally turned around from the jump seats and said to the president, "You can't say that Dallas isn't friendly to you today."

At approximately 12:30 P.M., the president's car passed an orange brick warehouse and office building, the Texas

School Book Depository. According to witnesses, several gunshots soon resounded in rapid succession. The president and Governor Connally were hit. A shot to the rear portion of Kennedy's head caused a massive wound. The president slumped into Mrs. Kennedy's lap.

Secret Service agent Clinton J. Hill ran from the follow-up car to the presidential limousine, where he shielded Mrs. Kennedy and the stricken president as the driver raced to Parkland Memorial Hospital. Despite attempts to save the president's life, by 1:00 P.M. all heart activity had ceased. Doctors pronounced the president dead.

On the day of the assassination, the police arrested twenty-four-year-old ex-marine Lee Harvey Oswald for the shooting and murder of officer J.D. Tippit of the Dallas Police. As eyewitnesses came forth and evidence was gathered, Oswald quickly became a suspect in the president's assassination. One eyewitness, Howard L. Brennan, claimed that a man matching Oswald's description was on the sixth floor of the Texas School Book Depository at the time of the shooting. The FBI traced a rifle found on the sixth floor of the depository back to Oswald, and Oswald was formally charged with the assassination of President Kennedy. Two days later, during his transport from the city jail to the Dallas County jail, Oswald himself was fatally shot in the basement of the Dallas police station by Jack Ruby, a nightclub owner.

## The Official Report

On November 24, 1963, Kennedy's successor, President Lyndon B. Johnson, appointed a seven-member commission, headed by U.S. Supreme Court chief justice Earl Warren, to conduct a thorough investigation of the assassination. The Warren Commission Report was released to the public on September 27, 1964. The 296,000-word report was based on the testimony of 552 witnesses taken over a period of several months. The report concluded that Lee Harvey Oswald was the one and only assassin and that there was no evidence of a conspiracy surrounding the assassination. The administration and the commission hoped that their lengthy investigative findings would put any wavering doubts to rest.

## The Skeptics

The publication of the Warren Report was soon followed by the publication of the twenty-six volumes of the com-

*President John F. Kennedy delivers a speech in Fort Worth, Texas, on the morning of November 22, 1963.*

mission's hearings. However, due to Cold War tensions and the perceived threat of communism, the U.S. government discouraged the release of certain documents surrounding the investigation, particularly those of the intelligence and security agencies. As a result, the official record on the assassination of President Kennedy remained a mystery.

The secrecy surrounding the investigation fueled speculation among the American people. Many believed that the Warren Commission had been predisposed to the "lone-assassin" theory and therefore did whatever it took to confirm this theory and subsequently put to rest any notions of a conspiracy. They also believed that the commission had been too dependent on the FBI and CIA for information.

The skeptics decided to begin their own investigations of the assassination. They searched for inconsistencies in the exhibits and testimony that were used by the Warren Commission during its investigation. For example, the Warren Report concluded that Oswald had the rifle in his possession on his way to work on the morning of the assassination; however, witnesses claimed that the package he carried was about two feet long, which was too short for a forty-inch rifle. In addition, there was an inconsistency regarding the identification of the alleged weapon used in the assassination. An officer at the scene identified the rifle as a German Mauser, when it was clearly labeled as a 6.5

Mannlicher-Carcano rifle made in Italy. This obvious discrepancy led to suspicions that the rifle was planted to frame Oswald as the killer.

These amateur researchers also compared the varied eyewitness testimonies regarding the source of the gunshots. One eyewitness, Malcolm Summer, who was standing on a nearby grassy knoll, stated, "I do think that the first shot came from the School Book Depository up there, and then when the second one came I did not know who all was shooting. I was thinking it was more than one person shooting. The first shot sounded just like a little pop, it sounded like a firecracker from a far away distance, the others sounded real close, real close." Eyewitness Bill Newman, who had been on the north side of Elm Street and was the closest spectator to the president when he was struck in the head stated that he believed the shots were coming from directly behind him (the knoll area). These eyewitness accounts implied that there was another shooter (or shooters) in addition to Oswald.

The medical evidence was another point of dispute among skeptics. Conflicting reports on the president's autopsy—specifically regarding where the wounds were located and which wounds were exit wounds versus entry wounds—increased suspicions. According to the Parkland Hospital doctors who performed the autopsy on Kennedy, the first bullet to hit the president entered at the front of his throat, immediately under his Adam's apple. Two weeks later, the FBI delivered a summary report to the Warren Commission. The report was not published, but a leak contradicted the Parkland Hospital doctors' report; the FBI claimed that the first bullet had made "a small, neat wound in the back and penetrated two or three inches." Many skeptics interpreted this contradiction in testimony concerning where and how the first bullet hit as evidence of a conspiracy.

Different theories rapidly spread throughout the public arena via books and various articles. Some theorists believed that the Mafia was involved in the assassination, particularly after it was discovered that Jack Ruby had ties to organized crime. Kennedy's shakedown of organized crime clearly gave the Mafia a motive to assassinate the president. Other skeptics thought high government officials linked to the military-industrial complex were responsible, their motive being to continue the war in Vietnam. Many believed that the commission's dependence on the FBI and CIA for information had thwarted the commission's ability to complete a thorough investigation since these agencies could have been covering up for the government. Others proposed the involvement of anti-Castro Cubans who still resented Kennedy for the failed 1961 Bay of Pigs invasion. They theorized that the Cuban exiles—who were trained by the CIA in an attempt to overthrow the regime of Fidel Castro—had a motive to kill Kennedy. Defenders of the Warren Commission, however, responded that omissions or contradictions in the report were best explained as human error, not intentional deceit.

## A Government Official Challenges the Official Report

In November 1966, Jim Garrison, then district attorney of New Orleans, joined the throngs of assassination buffs when he initiated his own investigation of the Kennedy assassination. Garrison's doubts about the Warren Report emerged after he analyzed the report and the volumes of evidence and testimony used by the commission. He believed that the commission simply had not had all the facts; the supposed "facts" it did have were fraudulent as a result of the CIA's withholding of evidence.

Garrison disputed the "lone-assassin" theory and proposed his own theory. He attempted to do this by refuting the Warren Report's conclusions regarding the number of bullets fired. The commission had concluded that three bullets were fired from the sixth floor of the book depository within a period of 5.6 seconds. The second bullet missed completely. The third bullet hit Kennedy in the back of the head, causing a massive, fatal wound. The first bullet, which supposedly caused nonfatal injuries to both Kennedy and Connally, is the source of much speculation. It is known as the "magic bullet" because of the implausibility of its course. According to the Warren Report, this bullet hit Kennedy in the back of his neck. Then, without striking any hard object, it passed through his neck to exit at the front of his throat. It then entered Connally's back at his right armpit, sliding along his fifth rib and demolishing four inches of the rib before it exited his chest below the right nipple. The bullet then struck and shattered the radius of

Connally's right wrist on the dorsal side, exited at the base of his palm, and then hit his left thigh close to his knee.

Not only did the mechanics of the bullet's journey seem implausible to Garrison but the bullet was in nearly pristine condition. There was no evidence that the bullet retrieved at the scene had ever impacted the body of any human being or penetrated any clothing at any time, much less specifically that of Kennedy and Connally. The angles of the entry wounds in Kennedy and Connally were markedly different, without adequate explanation.

Garrison rejected the commission's conclusions regarding this bullet. He insisted that the commission had produced the "magic bullet" scenario in order to bolster its lone gunman theory. If the commission had decided that separate bullets had struck Kennedy and Connally, it would have been forced to conclude that there had been a fourth bullet. And since there had not been enough time for Oswald to fire more than three shots, it would have meant that there was more than one gunman, a theory the commission emphatically denied.

Despite the large amount of criticism he received, Garrison maintained his position on the assassination and eventually put New Orleans businessman Clay Shaw on trial for the murder of John F. Kennedy. All charges against Shaw were eventually dropped, but Garrison pledged to continue his investigation: "As long as the men who shot John Kennedy to death in Dallas are walking the streets of America, I will continue this investigation." Jim Garrison died in 1995. He was the only person to ever bring someone to trial for the assassination of John F. Kennedy.

## Nagging Questions

More than a decade after the assassination and the Warren Report, doubts persisted among many Americans. Many people still believed that a conspiracy was involved in the assassination of Kennedy; they were not satisfied with the Warren Commission's findings. In September 1976, a resolution was passed to create a twelve-member select committee to investigate these lingering doubts. This committee, called the House Select Committee on Assassinations (HSCA), was mandated to investigate the circumstances surrounding the deaths of John F. Kennedy and Reverend Martin Luther King Jr. and the agencies of the U.S. government that were involved in the original investigations into those murders.

The HSCA determined that the Warren Commission had conducted a thorough and professional investigation into Lee Harvey Oswald's role in Kennedy's assassination but had failed to investigate the possibility of a conspiracy to assassinate the president. This deficiency, the HSCA stated, was partly due to the failure of the Warren Commission to obtain all the relevant information that was in the possession of other agencies and departments of the government. The HSCA also acknowledged the time pressures under which the Warren Commission investigation was conducted, which compromised its work product and conclusions.

The HSCA discovered substantive new information that the Warren Commission failed to thoroughly investigate, including Jack Ruby's associations with organized crime; the existence of CIA-Mafia assassination plots against Castro; specific threats against Kennedy that were identified by the Secret Service during 1963; and the violent attitude of powerful organized crime figures toward the president. The commission also failed to fully analyze all the available scientific evidence to determine the number of shots fired. In its final report, the HSCA found a "probable" conspiracy in the Kennedy assassination but was unable to determine the nature of the conspiracy or its participants other than Oswald.

In 1992 Oliver Stone's high-profile movie *JFK* was released to the general public. The film's premise of the probable conspiracy in the death of Kennedy piqued many people's interest. In response to the public's continued, heated speculation, Congress passed the President John F. Kennedy Assassination Records Collection Act of 1992, mandating the gathering and opening of all records concerned with the death of the president. Congress also established the Assassination Records Review Board to reexamine for release the records that the agencies still regarded as too sensitive to open to the public and to ensure that government agencies cooperated with the Kennedy act.

The Assassination Records Review Board had much success with its endeavors. Some of its major accomplishments included the acquiring of film footage depicting events surrounding the assassination; the release of all FBI and CIA documents from previous official investigations; the arrangement for the first known authenticity study of the film of the assassination; and the sponsorship of ballistics and forensic testing of the bullet fragment known as Warren Commission Exhibit 567, which, according to the commission, was from the third and final bullet that caused the fatal blow to the president's head.

Today, in the age of advanced technology, thousands of websites appear on the Internet full of information surrounding the assassination of John F. Kennedy. Skeptics and conspiracy theorists continue to seek new evidence to prove their theories. Books and articles by Kennedy researchers are bountiful as well, many claiming to have found the truth behind the assassination. Whatever the truth may be, it is clear that the event has captured the public's imagination and will likely remain a source of contentious debate for years to come.

# Chapter 1

# The Warren Report

# 1

# The Warren Report: One Gunman, Acting Alone, Shot and Killed the President

### The Warren Commission

On November 29, 1963, seven days after the tragic assassination of President John F. Kennedy, President Lyndon Johnson appointed a commission to investigate the circumstances surrounding both Kennedy's killing and that of the alleged assassin, Lee Harvey Oswald. The seven-member commission, headed by Chief Justice Earl Warren, was assisted by a large staff divided into teams to deal with the various subjects being investigated. The commission relied heavily on the Federal Bureau of Investigation for evidence throughout the investigation. On September 24, 1964, ten months after the Warren Commission began its investigation, it submitted a 296,000-word report based on the testimony of 552 witnesses. The main conclusions were that Lee Harvey Oswald was a lone assassin and that no evidence was found to suggest that Oswald or Jack Ruby, Oswald's killer, were part of any conspiracy to kill the president.

---

This Commission was created to ascertain the facts relating to the . . . events and to consider the important questions which they raised. The Commission has addressed itself to this task and has reached certain conclu-

The Warren Commission, "Report of the President's Commission on the Assassination of President Kennedy," *U.S. National Archives & Records Administration*, 1964, pp. 18–23.

sions based on all the available evidence. No limitations have been placed on the Commission's inquiry; it has conducted its own investigation, and all Government agencies have fully discharged their responsibility to cooperate with the Commission in its investigation. These conclusions represent the reasoned judgment of all members of the Commission and are presented after an investigation which has satisfied the Commission that it has ascertained the truth concerning the assassination of President Kennedy to the extent that a prolonged and thorough search makes this possible.

---

*The shots which killed President Kennedy and wounded Governor Connally were fired by Lee Harvey Oswald.*

---

1. The shots which killed President Kennedy and wounded Governor Connally were fired from the sixth floor window at the southeast corner of the Texas School Book Depository. This determination is based upon the following:
   - (a) Witnesses at the scene of the assassination saw a rifle being fired from the sixth floor window of the Depository Building, and some witnesses saw a rifle in the window immediately after the shots were fired.
   - (b) The nearly whole bullet found on Governor Connally's stretcher at Parkland Memorial Hospital and the two bullet fragments found in the front seat of the Presidential limousine were fired from the 6.5-millimeter Mannlicher-Carcano rifle found on the sixth floor of the Depository Building to the exclusion of all other weapons.
   - (c) The three used cartridge cases found near the window on the sixth floor at the southeast corner of the building were fired from the same rifle which fired the above-described bullet and fragments, to the exclusion of all other weapons.
   - (d) The windshield in the Presidential limousine was struck by a bullet fragment on the inside surface of the glass, but was not penetrated.
   - (e) The nature of the bullet wounds suffered by

President Kennedy and Governor Connally and the location of the car at the time of the shots establish that the bullets were fired from above and behind the Presidential limousine, striking the President and the Governor as follows:

1. President Kennedy was first struck by a bullet which entered at the back of his neck and exited through the lower front portion of his neck, causing a wound which would not necessarily have been lethal. The President was struck a second time by a bullet which entered the right-rear portion of his head, causing a massive and fatal wound.

2. Governor Connally was struck by a bullet which entered on the right side of his back and traveled downward through the right side of his chest, exiting below his right nipple. This bullet then passed through his right wrist and entered his left thigh where it caused a superficial wound.

- (f) There is no credible evidence that the shots were fired from the Triple Underpass, ahead of the motorcade, or from any other location.

---

*Oswald lied to the police after his arrest.*

---

2. The weight of the evidence indicates that there were three shots fired.

3. Although it is not necessary to any essential findings of the Commission to determine just which shot hit Governor Connally, there is very persuasive evidence from the experts to indicate that the same bullet which pierced the President's throat also caused Governor Connally's wounds. However, Governor Connally's testimony and certain other factors have given rise to some difference of opinion as to this probability but there is no question in the mind of any member of the Commission that all the shots which caused the President's and Governor Connally's wounds were fired from the sixth floor window of the Texas School Book Depository.

4. The shots which killed President Kennedy and wounded Governor Connally were fired by Lee Har-

vey Oswald. This conclusion is based upon the following:

- (a) The Mannlicher-Carcano 6.5-millimeter Italian rifle from which the shots were fired was owned by and in the possession of Oswald.
- (b) Oswald carried this rifle into the Depository Building on the morning of November 22, 1963.
- (c) Oswald, at the time of the assassination, was present at the window from which the shots were fired.
- (d) Shortly after the assassination, the Mannlicher-Carcano rifle belonging to Oswald was found partially hidden between some cartons on the sixth floor and the improvised paper bag in which Oswald brought the rifle to the Depository was found close by the window from which the shots were fired.
- (e) Based on testimony of the experts and their analysis of films of the assassination, the Commission has concluded that a rifleman of Lee Harvey Oswald's capabilities could have fired the shots from the rifle used in the assassination within the elapsed time of the shooting. The Commission has concluded further that Oswald possessed the capability with a rifle which enabled him to commit the assassination.
- (f) Oswald lied to the police after his arrest concerning important substantive matters.
- (g) Oswald had attempted to kill Maj. Gen. Edwin A. Walker (Retired, U.S. Army) on April 10, 1963, thereby demonstrating his disposition to take human life.

---

*[The information] helped to create doubts, speculations, and fears in the mind of the public.*

---

5. Oswald killed Dallas Police Patrolman J.D. Tippit approximately 45 minutes after the assassination. This conclusion upholds the finding that Oswald fired the shots which killed President Kennedy and wounded Governor Connally and is supported by the following:
- (a) Two eyewitnesses saw the Tippit shooting and seven eyewitnesses heard the shots and saw the

gunman leave the scene with revolver in hand. These nine eyewitnesses positively identified Lee Harvey Oswald as the man they saw.

- (b) The cartridge cases found at the scene of the shooting were fired from the revolver in the possession of Oswald at the time of his arrest to the exclusion of all other weapons.
- (c) The revolver in Oswald's possession at the time of his arrest was purchased by and belonged to Oswald.
- (d) Oswald's jacket was found along the path of flight taken by the gunman as he fled from the scene of the killing.

6. Within 80 minutes of the assassination and 35 minutes of the Tippit killing Oswald resisted arrest at the theatre by attempting to shoot another Dallas police officer.

---

*The Commission has found no evidence that Oswald was involved with any person or group in a conspiracy.*

---

7. The Commission has reached the following conclusions concerning Oswald's interrogation and detention by the Dallas police:
- (a) Except for the force required to effect his arrest, Oswald was not subjected to any physical coercion by any law enforcement officials. He was advised that he could not be compelled to give any information and that any statements made by him might be used against him in court. He was advised of his right to counsel. He was given the opportunity to obtain counsel of his own choice and was offered legal assistance by the Dallas Bar Association, which he rejected at that time.
- (b) Newspaper, radio, and television reporters were allowed uninhibited access to the area through which Oswald had to pass when he was moved from his cell to the interrogation room and other sections of the building, thereby subjecting Oswald to harassment and creating chaotic conditions which were not conducive to orderly interrogation

or the protection of the rights of the prisoner.
- (c) The numerous statements, sometimes erroneous, made to the press by various local law enforcement officials during this period of confusion and disorder in the police station would have presented serious obstacles to the obtaining of a fair trial for Oswald. To the extent that the information was erroneous or misleading, it helped to create doubts, speculations, and fears in the mind of the public which might otherwise not have arisen.

---

*On the basis of the evidence before the Commission it concludes that Oswald acted alone.*

---

8. The Commission has reached the following conclusions concerning the killing of Oswald by Jack Ruby on November 24, 1963:
- (a) Ruby entered the basement of the Dallas Police Department shortly after 11:17 A.M. and killed Lee Harvey Oswald at 11:21 A.M.
- (b) Although the evidence on Ruby's means of entry is not conclusive, the weight of the evidence indicates that he walked down the ramp leading from Main Street to the basement of the police department.
- (c) There is no evidence to support the rumor that Ruby may have been assisted by any members of the Dallas Police Department in the killing of Oswald.
- (d) The Dallas Police Department's decision to transfer Oswald to the county jail in full public view was unsound. The arrangements made by the police department on Sunday morning, only a few hours before the attempted transfer, were inadequate. Of critical importance was the fact that news media representatives and others were not excluded from the basement even after the police were notified of threats to Oswald's life. These deficiencies contributed to the death of Lee Harvey Oswald.
9. The Commission has found no evidence that either Lee Harvey Oswald or Jack Ruby was part of any conspiracy, domestic or foreign, to assassinate Presi-

dent Kennedy. The reasons for this conclusion are:
- (a) The Commission has found no evidence that anyone assisted Oswald in planning or carrying out the assassination. In this connection it has thoroughly investigated, among other factors, the circumstances surrounding the planning of the motorcade route through Dallas, the hiring of Oswald by the Texas School Book Depository Co. on October 15, 1963, the method by which the rifle was brought into the building, the placing of cartons of books at the window, Oswald's escape from the building, and the testimony of eyewitnesses to the shooting.
- (b) The Commission has found no evidence that Oswald was involved with any person or group in a conspiracy to assassinate the President, although it has thoroughly investigated, in addition to other possible leads, all facets of Oswald's associations, finances, and personal habits, particularly during the period following his return from the Soviet Union in June 1962.
- (c) The Commission has found no evidence to show that Oswald was employed, persuaded, or encouraged by any foreign government to assassinate President Kennedy or that he was an agent of any foreign government, although the Commission has reviewed the circumstances surrounding Oswald's defection to the Soviet Union, his life there from October of 1959 to June of 1962 so far as it can be reconstructed, his known contacts with the Fair Play for Cuba Committee and his visits to the Cuban and Soviet Embassies in Mexico City during his trip to Mexico from September 26 to October 3, 1963, and his known contacts with the Soviet Embassy in the United States.
- (d) The Commission has explored all attempts of Oswald to identify himself with various political groups, including the Communist Party, U.S.A., the Fair Play for Cuba Committee, and the Socialist Workers Party, and has been unable to find any evidence that the contacts which he initiated were related to Oswald's subsequent assassination of the President.

- (e) All of the evidence before the Commission established that there was nothing to support the speculation that Oswald was an agent, employee, or informant of the FBI, the CIA, or any other governmental agency. It has thoroughly investigated Oswald's relationships prior to the assassination with all agencies of the U.S. Government. All contacts with Oswald by any of these agencies were made in the regular exercise of their different responsibilities.
- (f) No direct or indirect relationship between Lee Harvey Oswald and Jack Ruby has been discovered by the Commission, nor has it been able to find any credible evidence that either knew the other, although a thorough investigation was made of the many rumors and speculations of such a relationship.
- (g) The Commission has found no evidence that Jack Ruby acted with any other person in the killing of Lee Harvey Oswald.
- (h) After careful investigation the Commission has found no credible evidence either that Ruby and Officer Tippit, who was killed by Oswald, knew each other or that Oswald and Tippit knew each other.

Because of the difficulty of proving negatives to a certainty the possibility of others being involved with either Oswald or Ruby cannot be established categorically, but if there is any such evidence it has been beyond the reach of all the investigative agencies and resources of the United States and has not come to the attention of this Commission.

10. In its entire investigation the Commission has found no evidence of conspiracy, subversion, or disloyalty to the U.S. Government by any Federal, State, or local official.
11. On the basis of the evidence before the Commission it concludes that Oswald acted alone. Therefore, to determine the motives for the assassination of President Kennedy, one must look to the assassin himself. Clues to Oswald's motives can be found in his family history, his education or lack of it, his acts, his writings, and the recollections of those who had

close contacts with him throughout his life. The Commission has presented with this report all of the background information bearing on motivation which it could discover. Thus, others may study Lee Oswald's life and arrive at their own conclusions as to his possible motives.

The Commission could not make any definitive determination of Oswald's motives. It has endeavored to isolate factors which contributed to his character and which might have influenced his decision to assassinate President Kennedy. These factors were:

- (a) His deep-rooted resentment of all authority which was expressed in a hostility toward every society in which he lived;
- (b) His inability to enter into meaningful relationships with people, and a continuous pattern of rejecting his environment in favor of new surrounding;
- (c) His urge to try to find a place in history and despair at times over failures in his various undertakings;
- (d) His capacity for violence as evidenced by his attempt to kill General Walker;
- (e) His avowed commitment to Marxism and communism, as he understood the terms and developed his own interpretation of them; this was expressed by his antagonism toward the United States, by his defection to the Soviet Union, by his failure to be reconciled with life in the United States even after his disenchantment with the Soviet Union, and by his efforts, though frustrated, to go to Cuba.

Each of these contributed to his capacity to risk all in cruel and irresponsible actions.

# 2

# The Commission Used Unsound Tactics in the Case Against Oswald

Leo Sauvage

In this article written in 1965, Leo Sauvage, one of France's most distinguished writers and author of the book *L'Affaire Oswald*, closely examines the evidence that the Warren Commission used to prove Lee Harvey Oswald's guilt. In the report the commission omitted certain details from the statements made by M.N. McDonald, the officer who initially took Oswald into custody from the Texas Theater. McDonald stated that Oswald, upon his arrest, "remained seated without moving, just looking at me." In this testimony, Sauvage argues, Oswald fits the profile of a calm, innocent man. The Warren Commission only made use of the statements that could implicate Oswald as the assassin. McDonald explained that when he started to search for a weapon on the suspect, Oswald punched him in the face—the Warren Commission used this action as proof of guilt, but according to Sauvage it was merely an ineffective act of irrational anger, not necessarily guilt. Sauvage also points out the Warren Commission's blatant manipulation of eyewitness testimony. The two eyewitness accounts of the brown paper bag carried by Oswald, which allegedly held the dismantled rifle, were applicable only to a package that could not have possibly contained the rifle. The Warren Commission proceeded to claim that the eyewitnesses were mistaken in their descriptions and concluded that the brown paper bag could have contained the weapon.

Leo Sauvage, "The Warren Commission's Case Against Oswald," *The New Leader*, November 22, 1965, pp. 16–21. Copyright © 1965 by The American Labor Conference on International Affairs, Inc. Reproduced by permission.

The [Warren] Commission insists it did not pass judgment on [Lee Harvey] Oswald. According to its Report, it merely "ascertained the facts surrounding the assassination but did not draw conclusions concerning Oswald's legal guilt." It was content simply to gather the evidence which "identifies Lee Harvey Oswald as the assassin of President [John F.] Kennedy." Judgment or not, no American newspaper that I know of today feels obliged to place the word "alleged" before "assassin" in referring to Oswald.

On what grounds does the Commission, headed by the Chief Justice of the United States, label as an assassin a man whom it claims not to be judging and whose family, for that reason, was refused an opportunity to defend his name? A summary of its indictment is presented at the conclusion of Chapter IV of the Report, which is titled, precisely, "The Assassin":

> "The Commission has found that Lee Harvey Oswald 1) owned and possessed the rifle used to kill President Kennedy and wound [Texas] Governor [John] Connally, 2) brought this rifle into the Depository Building on the morning of the assassination, 3) was present, at the time of the assassination, at the window from which the shots were fired, 4) killed Dallas Police Officer J.D. Tippit in an apparent attempt to escape, 5) resisted arrest by drawing a fully loaded pistol and attempting to shoot another police officer, 6) lied to the police after his arrest concerning important substantive matters, 7) attempted, in April 1963, to kill Maj. General Edwin A. Walker, and 8) possessed the capability with a rifle which would have enabled him to commit the assassination. On the basis of these findings the Commission has concluded that Lee Harvey Oswald was the assassin of President Kennedy.". . .

## Oswald's "Lies"

To begin with, it is necessary to single out proof number 6, concerning Oswald's "lies." I use quotations around the word "lies" because it is a reference to statements of the accused which, since they were not recorded on tape or by a stenographer, are known to us only through the recollections of various policemen who questioned Oswald. While the Commission apparently sees nothing reprehensible in that fact (it is also not shocked that the man suspected of having killed the President of the United States was questioned for a total of 12 hours in the absence of a lawyer), it is certainly not regular procedure to hold a defendant accountable for remarks attributed to him by his interrogators when it is impossible to know their context and still less their exact terms. . . .

In addition, it certainly cannot be presumed that Oswald believed he was obliged to tell the truth to hostile police whom he scorned and blamed for not providing him with a lawyer; as the Report says, he was "overbearing and arrogant throughout much of the time between his arrest and his own death."

---

*It certainly cannot be presumed that Oswald believed he was obliged to tell the truth.*

---

It seems clear to me, given these circumstances, that proof number 6 proves nothing. Indeed, it is rather astonishing that the Commission dared to include Oswald's "lies" as one of its eight officially proclaimed proofs on page 195 of the Report, for on page 180 it declares: "Oswald's untrue statements during interrogation were not considered items of positive proof by the Commission."

Three other affirmations of the Commission—numbers 4, 5 and 7—appear to have no genuine connection with its conclusion. Number 4, for example, rests essentially on such a scandalous collection of inacceptable "testimony" and inadmissible "identification" that it constitutes a graver indictment of the Commission than of Oswald. But let us suppose, for a moment, that the accusation was based on valid arguments. It would still be necessary to show how his murdering [officer J.D.] Tippit proved that Oswald was Kennedy's assassin.

## The Murder of J.D. Tippit

The Commission's explanation is that Oswald killed Tippit "in an apparent attempt to escape." Yet, no one—the Commission no more than I—knows why Tippit, alone in his patrol car, "pulled up alongside a man walking in the same direction." The Commission states that "it is conceivable, even probable, that Tippit stopped Oswald because of the description broadcast by the police radio." This statement is ridiculous. The description broadcast by the police did not mention clothing, shoes, manner or any other distinctive trait enabling identification of a man approached from behind in a car. And this occurred several miles from the scene of the crime, in a neighborhood where Tippit (unless he was informed about Oswald, a hypothesis the Commission avoids like the plague) had no reason to seek the suspect. . . .

---

*The circumstances of Oswald's arrest in the Texas Theater remain confused.*

---

Is it "probable," even "conceivable," that in the entire Dallas Police Department, J.D. Tippit alone was able to identify someone he saw from behind, in Oak Cliff, who in fact stood 5 foot 9 inches tall, was 24 years old, and weighed between 140 and 150 pounds? Finally, according to the extraordinary Helen Markham—whose testimony the Commission regards as "reliable," though I do not have the slightest faith in it—Tippit did not at any time act as if he were dealing with someone suspected of assassinating the President. In short, it is impossible to affirm that Oswald was seeking "to escape" because it is impossible to affirm that Tippit was trying to arrest him.

## Resisting Arrest

Nor is it possible to affirm, as proof number 5 does, that Oswald "resisted arrest by drawing a fully loaded pistol and attempting to shoot another police officer." The circumstances of Oswald's arrest in the Texas Theater remain confused, since the Warren Report does not elucidate any of the contradictions and inconsistencies raised by the accounts of the police officers, and the two witnesses it produced (out of a total it estimates at 12 or 14) only added new contradictions and inconsistencies, as the Commission recognizes. The Report itself, and the statements of officer M.N. McDonald contained in Volume III of the Hearings of the Commission, show that in striking the officer who was arresting him, Oswald was not attempting an escape. Oswald resisted arrest, the Report tells us, by hitting McDonald "between the eyes with his left fist," and it was only after this, according to the Report, that he drew a gun.

If Oswald had wanted to "shoot another police officer," he had plenty of time to do so, since McDonald—even though the suspect had been immediately pointed out to him in the back of the theater—first searched "two men in the center of the main floor, about ten rows from the front." McDonald acknowledged that during this time Oswald "remained seated without moving, just looking at me." Later, when questioned by Senator John Sherman Cooper (R-Ky.), who was clearly intrigued, McDonald repeated a second time that Oswald "just sat in his seat, with his hands on his lap, watching me." The Report does not reproduce these embarrassing details from the hearings, but it does not hesitate to state that when McDonald finally decided to approach Oswald, the latter "rose from his seat, bringing up both hands." There was thus no question of Oswald's resisting arrest even at this final moment, and it was only when "McDonald started to search Oswald's waist for a gun" that the man presented to us as the calm killer of President Kennedy and Officer Tippit ventures his first gesture of resistance: a punch in the face.

## In furtherance of which beliefs is Oswald supposed to have slain Kennedy?

While resistance to arrest is considered an incriminating circumstance, it is not proof of guilt. When such resistance reveals neither premeditation nor method but actually appears to be an ineffective act of irrational anger, it actually often constitutes an indication of innocence.

As for proof number 7 . . . suffice to say that the accusation rests essentially on the "revelations" of Marina Oswald [the widow of Lee Harvey Oswald]—whom everyone need not regard with the same confident admiration as does Justice Warren. Besides, her testimony is contradicted by a mountain of improbabilities: the circumstances under which Oswald would have been able to go to Walker's house and back, the identification of the recovered bullet, the simple fact that the sharpshooter of Elm Street is supposed to have missed an extremely easy target and, curiously, did not immediately fire a second shot. All that matters here, however, is the way the Commission tries to link the [April 1963] attack on Walker with the President's assassination.

## Oswald's Beliefs and Capabilities

The idea, apparently, is that the attempt on Walker demonstrates Oswald's "disposition to take human life" and "his capacity for violence." This is summed up in Chapter VII of the Report, where "possible motives" of Oswald are discussed, in a striking sentence that is in itself sufficient to destroy proof number 7: "The Commission has concluded that on April 10, 1963, Oswald shot at Maj. General Edwin A. Walker (Retired U.S. Army), demonstrating once again his propensity to act dramatically and, in this instance, violently, in furtherance of his beliefs."

In furtherance of which beliefs is Oswald supposed to have slain Kennedy? The Report gives us the following details: "Oswald did not lack the determination and other traits required to carry out a carefully planned killing of another human being and was willing to consummate such a purpose if he thought there was sufficient reason to do so. Some idea of what he thought was sufficient reason for such an act may be found in the nature of the motive that he stated for his attack on General Walker. Marina Oswald indicated that her husband had compared General Walker to Adolph [*sic*] Hitler . . ." Granting for now, as does Chief Justice Warren, that the word of Marina Oswald is sacred—did Oswald consider John Kennedy to be another Hitler or another Walker? Oswald's various statements about Kennedy, cited by the Report, categorically disprove this interpretation; yet in the conclusion to Chapter VII the Commission coolly repeats that Oswald demonstrated "a capacity to act decisively and without regard to the consequences when such action would further his aims of the moment." Since one searches in vain, from start to finish of the Warren Report, for a single word on the "aims of the moment" Oswald believed he would serve by killing Kennedy, the Commission—to the extent that it brings up the attempt on Walker—seems to prove, if anything, that Oswald could not have been the assassin of President Kennedy.

## Ownership of the Rifle

Four affirmations remain which, according to the Commission, accuse and (if we can stop playing with words) condemn Oswald not by implication but directly. I am not going to discuss the ownership of the rifle (proof number 1), although I wonder what the Commission means by "possession." If it means that Oswald had the rifle in his possession at the moment of the crime, it would be necessary *first* to prove Affirmations 2 and 3: that Oswald had brought the rifle to the Depository on the morning of November 22, and that he was the man at the window on the sixth floor. If the Commission means that Oswald had uninterrupted possession of the rifle until the day of the crime, its own Report clearly establishes the shakiness of this contention. The Report does declare that "the rifle was kept among Oswald's possessions from the time of its purchase until the day of the assassination," but this statement is knowingly false. On the next page, in fact, the Commission states that its star witness, Marina Oswald, saw the stock of the rifle in the Paine garage at Irving [Texas] "about one week after the return from New Orleans," that is, about September 30. Two pages further, in describing the discovery of the empty blanket after 3 P.M. on November 22, the Report informs us that Marina Oswald testified that this was her first knowledge that the rifle was not in its accustomed place." Thus, according to the Commission's own Marina, the rifle could have disappeared from the unlocked garage of the Paine house without anyone noticing it at any time between September 30 and November 22, 1963, and the Report is overtly misleading in suggesting that the rifle was brought out of the garage only on "the morning of the assassination"—that is to say, in Oswald's package.

## Analysis of the Bullet Fragments

In any case, the Commission fails to prove that this rifle, however it arrived in the Depository, was "used to kill President Kennedy and wound Governor Connally." The Report offers us the testimony of experts who, basing their views on ballistics tests, affirm that two bullet fragments found in the front seat "after the Presidential car was returned to Washington" were fired from Oswald's Mannlicher-Carcano. One of the fragments represented less than a third, the other hardly more than an eighth of a complete bullet. They were mutilated to the point that "it was not possible to determine whether they were from the same bullet or from two different bullets," but the experts claim that each had a sufficient unmutilated area to provide the basis for identification. I will merely note that the manual on "Modern Criminal Investigations" by Harry Söderman and John J. O'Connell, in common use in American police academies, considers ballistics tests suitable for identification purposes only "if the bullet has retained its shape or is only partly deformed."

---

*The Commission fails to prove that this rifle . . . was "used to kill President Kennedy."*

---

There also exists, meanwhile, a "nearly whole bullet." Here the Commission would have had a better case if it did not ask us to believe that this bullet, after passing through the neck of the President, also passed through the Governor's chest, "shattering his fifth rib," and then traveled on through his right wrist, shedding small fragments of metal "upon striking the firm surface of the bone," and finally leaving "a tiny metallic fragment embedded in the Governor's leg"—all of this while remaining "nearly whole." The "nearly whole bullet," we are further told, was "slightly flattened but otherwise unmutilated.". . .

It must be noted, at least, that the Commission theory was rejected by several medical experts whose depositions are reproduced in the Hearings record even though they are ignored in the Report. In addition, while the Report rather arbitrarily affirms the existence of "very persuasive evidence from the experts to indicate that the same bullet which pierced the President's throat also caused Governor Connally's wounds," it does not conceal the formal disagreement of Connally himself and grants that "Governor Connally's testimony and other factors have given rise to some difference of opinion as to this probability." The Commission thus officially admits that this is not a demonstrated fact but a simple "probability," and a doubtful "probability" at that. . . .

## The Brown Paper Bag

Compromised already by the yawning gap, the fundamental accusation of the Warren Commission is definitely demolished by the fact that it is equally incapable of furnishing any evidence of the indispensable corollary: If Oswald's rifle was in fact the murder weapon, it is necessary to prove that it was Oswald who fired it. Countless crimes have been committed with weapons belonging to others, often precisely in order to incriminate the owners. The Commission carefully avoids any allusion to this possibility in the Oswald case, and to dodge this argument it employs affirmations 2 and 3. What remains of these after a close scrutiny?

Only two witnesses saw the brown paper package that Lee Oswald carried when he went to work on the morning of November 22—the package which, the Commission says, contained the dismantled rifle. In their deposition before the Commission on March 11, 1964, Wesley Frazier and Linnie Mae Randle were exhaustively questioned by Assistant Counsel Joseph A. Ball, who the Hearings record shows, employed the traps and tricks and other devices an experienced lawyer makes use of when testimony embarrasses him. This effort was a total loss, however: The descriptions given by Frazier and Mrs. Randle, confirmed by the practical tests to which the witnesses were put by Ball, applied to a package which could not have contained the rifle. Does the Commission waver? No: "The Commission has weighed the visual recollection of Frazier and Mrs. Randle against the evidence here presented that the bag Oswald carried contained the assassination weapon and has concluded that Frazier and Mrs. Randle are mistaken as to the length of the bag.". . .

## Manipulation of Testimony

It is now necessary to discuss proof number 3—the testimony of Howard L. Brennan, which the Commission uses as the basis for stating that Oswald "was present, at the time of the assassination, at the window from which the shots were fired."

---

*Countless crimes have been committed with weapons belonging to others.*

---

Howard L. Brennan—one of the Commission's star witnesses, along with Marina Oswald and Helen Markham—was presented as an apparent discovery of the Commission. Yet Brennan's statements had appeared in the press from the start of the investigation in Dallas. Nobody at that time took him seriously, and it was necessary to await the Warren Report to learn that "Howard L. Brennan made a positive identification of Oswald as being the person at the window." Leafing back in the Report to the chapter on "The Assas-

sin," and its section titled "Eyewitness Identification of Assassin," we learn that "Brennan testified that the man in the
window was standing when he fired the shots," while the
Report is obliged to recognize that "the half-open window,
the arrangement of the boxes, and the angle of the shots virtually preclude a standing position." The conclusion of the
Commission is that Brennan was mistaken in saying that the
man was standing, but not mistaken in identifying (from the
sidewalk opposite the building) the man sitting behind a
half-open sixth-floor window.

---

*Prior to the lineup, Brennan had seen Oswald's
picture.*

---

As to the variations which marked his identification in
the police lineup and the turnabouts that followed, these are
related on an epic page of the Report, the farcical torment of
which could never be suggested by any summary. I would
therefore refer the reader to page 145, only remarking that
one will also find there the following admission: "Prior to the
lineup, Brennan had seen Oswald's picture on television."

## The Sharpshooter

There remains affirmation number 8, the most dubious of
all, with the Commission serving up the refutation on a
large platter. To demonstrate Oswald's "rifle capability," the
Commission cites his record in the Marines: "Oswald was
tested in December of 1956, and obtained a score of 212,
which was 2 points above the minimum for qualification as
a 'sharpshooter' in a scale of marksman-sharpshooter-
expert. In May of 1959, on another range, Oswald scored
191, which was 1 point over the minimum for ranking as a
'marksman.'" To the layman, this suggests that Oswald was
among the elite riflemen of the U.S. Marine Corps, although his skill diminished somewhat between 1956 and
1959. What the Commission does not point out is that the
scale "marksman-sharpshooter-expert" applies not to an
elite group but to all Marines. Thus, toward the end of his
service, in May 1959, Oswald was just 1 point above the
minimum required of any one of the 175,571 Marines in the
Corps at that time. . . .

The only possible remedy, under these conditions, was

to demonstrate that nothing was easier than to obtain three direct hits in 4.8 to 5.6 seconds, with a bolt action rifle such as Oswald's Mannlicher-Carcano. And the Commission seems to have had no trouble in finding a Marine Sergeant, even a Marine Major, as well as an FBI expert and the "chief of the U.S. Army Infantry Weapons Evaluation Branch of the Ballistics Research Laboratory," to confirm this. But many European experts—including the Olympic rifle champion and instructors of the Italian Army, where the Mannlicher-Carcano was used during the War—continue to maintain the contrary. The Commission then asked three "masters" of the National Rifle Association—three recognized champions—to fire from the top of a tower with Oswald's rifle, at stationary targets at distances corresponding to those on Elm Street. The "chief of the U.S. Army Infantry Weapons Evaluation Branch of the Ballistics Research Laboratory" was asked to evaluate the results. And the chief, etc., testified in effect "that in his opinion the probability of hitting the targets at the relatively short range at which they were hit was very high.". . .

## The Non-Expert Oswald

It is clear that even if the three "masters" of the National Rifle Association—all of them identified in the Hearings as professional specialists—had done as well or better than the Elm Street assassin, that would prove little about non-expert Oswald. Moreover, contrary to the Report's claim, the conditions of the test did not "simulate those which prevailed during the assassination," since not only were the targets stationary but the champions "took as much time as they wanted for the first target," whereas the gunman of the Texas School Book Depository, by reason of the limitations imposed by the movement of the motorcade and by his own position at the window, had as little time for the first shot as for the two others. Despite all this, only one of the three "masters" matched the assassin.

How, under these circumstances, can the Warren Commission unhesitatingly assert that "Lee Harvey Oswald was the assassin of President Kennedy"?

# 3

# Weak Links in the Warren Report

Gerald Posner

Gerald Posner, a former Wall Street lawyer, examines the areas where he believes the Warren Report failed, areas that resulted in public criticism. Posner argues that the FBI and CIA both withheld information from the Warren Commission that was necessary to its investigation. The FBI deleted an agent's name from Oswald's address book that blatantly connected Oswald to the bureau. Potentially useful information about a conspiracy between the CIA and the Mafia to kill Fidel Castro was also kept from the commission. Contradictory autopsy reports and inadequate reenactments of the assassination weakened the credibility of the Warren Report, inciting an onslaught of conspiracy theorists. Posner argues that many later claims of amateur sleuths could have been avoided if the Warren Commission had been able to conduct a more thorough investigation.

The Warren Commission had its first meeting on December 5, 1963, only two weeks after the assassination, and four days later the FBI presented its five-volume report that summarized the Bureau's preliminary findings. Marina Oswald, the first witness, appeared on February 3, 1964. The Commission and its staff took testimony from 552 witnesses during the next six months. [Chief Justice Earl] Warren was so sensitive to possible government abuse that he established strict rules for the questioning of witnesses, in-

Gerald Posner, *Case Closed*. New York: Random House, 1993. Copyright © 1993 by Random House, Inc. Reproduced by permission.

cluding no private interrogations without a stenographer present and no polygraphs. . . .

The FBI's field investigation was, by itself, enormous. It conducted some 25,000 interviews and submitted over 2,300 investigative reports, totaling more than 25,000 pages. At the same time, the Secret Service conducted another 1,500 interviews and submitted 800 reports. Though many critics of the Warren Commission acknowledge that a mammoth examination was accomplished in a relatively brief period, they charge the Commission favored witnesses and documents that supported its early conclusion that Oswald alone killed the President. Yet this view underestimates the independence the legal staff had within the Commission's hierarchy. The staff could call any witness it wanted, and none of its more than 400 requests were ever denied by the commissioners.

## The FBI Withholds Information

The original deadline of June 30, 1964, turned out to be impractical. LBJ [President Lyndon Johnson], fearful that rumors might start that he had political reasons for delaying the report, wanted the work finished before the presidential nominating conventions. Warren told the other members, in a January 21 executive session, that it "would be very bad for the country to have this thing discussed" during the coming campaign. Tempers often flared during the final months as Warren pushed the probe at a pace that meant fourteen-hour days, seven days a week, for the legal staff. The 888-page final report was released three months late, on September 24, 1964.

---

*They charge the Commission favored witnesses and documents that supported its early conclusion.*

---

Although the Commission had done an extraordinary job of marshaling information and presenting it in a cohesive and organized manner, in only ten months it was not possible to delve into many issues that would later come to the forefront as nagging and persistent problems. Since it was so limited in manpower, the Commission was almost entirely dependent on agencies such as the FBI to conduct the actual investigation. [Senior member of the commission's general counsel, General J. Lee] Rankin had referred to "tender spots," potential embarrassments to the FBI or CIA that might hinder the sharing of information. J. Edgar Hoover was convinced within days of the assassination that Oswald alone had killed Kennedy. He knew, of course, that if Oswald was part of a conspiracy, the Bureau's reputation would suffer for not having uncovered the plot prior to JFK's trip to Dallas. Because of his iron-clad control over the Bureau, his feelings on the case colored the work the field agents did. Since Hoover thought the answer to the assassination was straightforward, he believed the Warren Commission could only cause problems by delving into many other areas. The FBI did not treat the Commission as its partner in search of the truth.

---

*The FBI even created files on the Commission's staff members.*

---

"I don't have any doubt that the FBI viewed the Commission the same way they later viewed civilians requesting documents," says James Lesar, the nation's leading attorney in pursuing assassination-related documents under the Freedom of Information Act (FOIA). The FBI even created files on the Commission's staff members. Richard Helms [former CIA director] later admitted that he only told the Warren Commission something if they asked for it. "I am sure the Bureau had the same attitude," says Lesar. "Basically, any request that comes in from a government commission or a citizen, the Bureau looks at very carefully to see if they can avoid responding. The relationship between the Commission and the Bureau was partly adversarial, because no one wanted to bring that tension out into the open. The Commission gave in to the FBI. In the executive sessions, they said they were going to investigate Hoover, but they knew they wouldn't."

## CIA Conspiracies Beneath the Surface

The FBI's early insistence that [Lee Harvey] Oswald was the lone assassin was actually a sore point with the Commission's staff. On January 22, 1964, Lee Rankin complained to the commissioners, "They [the FBI] would have us fold up and quit. . . . They found the man [Oswald]. There is nothing more to do. The Commission supports their conclusions, and we can go home and that is the end of it."

The FBI, anxious to downplay its contacts with Oswald, withheld information from the Commission, including Agent James Hosty's receipt of a note from Oswald. It also deleted Hosty's name, address, and telephone number, which were in Oswald's address book, when the information was sent to the Commission staff. The CIA withheld information as well, most critically that the Agency and the mafia had embarked on a joint effort to kill [Cuban premier] Fidel Castro.

"It's a serious point," says former staff lawyer Burt Griffin, now a judge. "I don't know if anyone will ever get the answer. I am not convinced, as I look back on it now, that Lee Rankin did not know about the CIA conspiracies to kill Castro. I don't have any evidence, but as I look back on the failure to bring us together to speculate, he never encouraged us to think speculatively, and the way Rankin operated with his door always closed, maybe he knew something and it was this secret. Only [Lyndon] Johnson, obviously, the Chief Justice, [former CIA director] Allen Dulles, and [Defense Secretary] Bobby Kennedy knew about the CIA plots against Castro. Its disclosure would have had very important implications. It might have allowed us to say something reasonably definitive about Oswald's motive. It would have put a new dimension on his Cuban activities and opened new areas of exploration. The fact that we could not come up with a motive for Oswald was a great weakness in the report."

---

*"We could not come up with a motive for Oswald."*

---

CBS news anchor Walter Cronkite summarized the concern of many when he noted that the FBI and CIA, by withholding information that later became public, "weakened the credibility of the Warren Report." But beyond the problems caused by its tug-of-war with the investigative branches, the Commission created many of its own difficulties. At the time, the Commission wanted to use the autopsy photos and X rays as the best evidence of how the President was shot, but the Kennedy family refused to release them.

Warren feared that if the Commission had the photos, they might be leaked to the press, and as a result he was hesitant to pressure Robert Kennedy on the matter. But Howard Willens, a staff attorney, had worked for Robert Kennedy and persisted to obtain them. In June 1964, RFK allowed only Warren and Rankin to review them. In his memoirs, Warren wrote, "[T]hey were so horrible that I could not sleep well for nights." None of the other commissioners or staff ever saw the autopsy photographs or X rays, nor did the panel utilize independent forensics experts. Reproduced in the final report are schematic drawings of the President's neck and head wounds, but both were made by an artist who was unfamiliar with the autopsy and never saw the photographs. The artist's sketches were based upon Drs. [James J.] Hume and [J. Thornton] Boswell's original measurements of the wounds. Those drawings were mistaken in the placement of both entry wounds, and that later developed into a significant issue for the conspiracy press.

## The Single-Bullet Theory

In other areas, the Commission's work seemed to stop just short of thoroughness. In replicating the firing of the Carcano [rifle], and figuring trajectory angles, the Commission used FBI tests that had a platform at the incorrect height when compared to the sixth floor of the Book Depository. The tests also calculated the minimum firing time and accuracy by shooting at stationary targets as opposed to a moving one such as Oswald had faced.

The single-bullet theory was not the result of positive evidence that clearly established it but an attempt to create a scenario to fit the facts as the Commission determined them. Unless one bullet caused the wounds to both Governor [John] Connally and President Kennedy, the Commission could not figure out how Oswald could have fired the three shots within the approximately five seconds they mistakenly allotted to him. Though advances in neutron activation and photographic and computer techniques now confirm that the theory is correct, the Commission had no way of being certain the single bullet was viable. The members were almost evenly split in their feelings about the theory, and Senator [Richard] Russell threatened not to sign a final report that absolutely concluded the single bullet was correct. They fought over the right adjective to use to describe the probability that the single bullet was right. [Commission member John J.] McCloy suggested "persuasive" evidence, while Russell wanted "credible" evidence, and [member Gerald] Ford pushed for "compelling." The Warren Commission Report settled on "There is very persuasive evidence." This type of compromise opened more doors to critics.

---

*The Commission's work seemed to stop just short of thoroughness.*

---

Few of the witnesses who contradicted the official version of events testified before the Commission. If they had been examined, their testimony would have been explainable, but because the Commission ignored them, critics had ammunition for future claims of deliberate omission. Also, the Commission underplayed Jack Ruby's underworld associations and did not effectively portray him as the unbalanced and volatile person he was, leaving itself open to criticism that it had failed to pursue the Ruby clues because it feared where those might lead. . . .

## The Commission Speaks Too Soon

But the most controversial aspect of the Commission's work may be its conclusion about the possibility of any conspiracy. The final report stated, "The Commission has found no evidence that either Lee Harvey Oswald or Jack Ruby was part of any conspiracy, domestic or foreign, to assassinate President Kennedy."

"There is no question Oswald was the shooter, and Oswald was the lone shooter," says former staff lawyer Burt Griffin. "We were wrong, in my opinion, in issuing the statement that there was no evidence of a conspiracy. That was the wrong statement. I frankly was very critical of using that language. There is plenty of evidence in the testimony and the documents that could lead a reasonable person to pursue a conspiracy theory. There is nothing that then establishes a conspiracy theory, but there is plenty there that would allow a reasonable person to speculate about a conspiracy theory. Statements like that sweeping 'no conspiracy' one does a disservice to our overall work. I think I was in a minority of one on that statement."

Despite its shortcomings, early reviews in the United

States generally lavished praise on the Warren Report. In Europe, however, where political conspiracies and government changeovers by violence are an integral part of much longer histories, the Commission's work was viewed as the official, sanitized version. Many leading European commentators questioned its conclusions without ever reading the report.

In the U.S., the honeymoon for critical acceptance was shortlived. By the time the Warren Commission published its report in September 1964, a network of amateur sleuths was prepared to check its accuracy against the research they had compiled since the day of the murder. An eclectic mixture of people across the country, many of whom were admitted leftists and were suspicious that a Communist was blamed for the murder in a right-wing city, had independently begun collecting everything printed on the subject. They also interviewed eyewitnesses and others connected to the case. Each soon carved out a specialty. . . .

## The Attack of the Critics

The earliest books [challenging the Warren Report] focused on apparent contradictions and unanswered questions in the report, such as the misidentification of the rifle found at the Depository as a Mauser instead of a Mannlicher-Carcano, or whether the man photographed standing in the doorway of the Depository during the assassination was Lee Oswald or his co-worker Billy Lovelady. Although the issues raised now seem rudimentary, they were the first to undermine the authority the press had bestowed on the Warren Commission. . . .

In its own reexamination of the case in the late 1970s, the House Select Committee investigated the first generation of critics and found their work wanting in terms of fairness and accuracy. Robert Blakey, the Select Committee's chief counsel, said that many early critics "had special axes to grind. As a result of our investigation, the Committee found that 'criticism leveled at the Commission . . . [was] often biased, unfair and inaccurate . . . [and] . . . the prevailing opinion of the Commission's performance was undeserved.'". . .

[Nevertheless] . . . those books were uniformly virulent attacks on the Warren Commission, and their advocacy often diminished their effectiveness. At their best, the critics had only exposed the Commission as incompetent, but they had not established it was wrong in its conclusions.

# 4

# Shifting Testimony Clouds the Report

Matthew Smith

Matthew Smith, a John F. Kennedy assassination researcher
from Sheffield, England, explores contradictions and discrep-
ancies he finds in the Warren Report regarding Lee Harvey
Oswald. Smith claims that the Warren Report is one-sided and
that the commission went to great lengths to support the
"lone-nut" killer theory. He examines, for instance, the eyewitness account of Howard L. Brennan, who testified that he
saw the assassin "standing" at the window. Smith argues that
because the window was open at the bottom only, a sniper
standing upright would have had to shoot through the glass.
The commission later contradicted its eyewitness, claiming
that Brennan must have been confused and instead saw the
shooter kneeling or squatting at the window. Police officials,
following Brennan's statement, had broadcast a description of
the suspect's height and weight to patrol cars. Viewing Oswald
in a police lineup that same day, Brennan was unable to make
a positive identification. Smith also tackles the contradictory
testimony surrounding the rifle found in the Texas School
Book Depository. The officers who discovered the rifle initially identified it as a German 7.65 Mauser—even though the
rifle butt was clearly marked "Made in Italy"—and only later
logged it as an Italian 6.5 Mannlicher-Carcano. Lee Harvey
Oswald owned an Italian 6.5 Mannlicher-Carcano.

According to the Warren Report, Lee Harvey Oswald
strolled out of the front door of the School Book De-

Matthew Smith, *JFK: The Second Plot*. London: Mainstream Publishing, 1992.
Copyright © 1992 by Matthew Smith. Reproduced by permission.

pository building and made his way to his lodgings, starting the journey by bus and transferring to a taxi when the bus got bogged down in the traffic chaos which followed in the wake of the assassination. Incredibly, he reached the rooming house at which he lived at a little before 1 P.M., less than 30 minutes after the shots were fired at the President. His time of arrival was confirmed by Earlene Roberts, who ran the establishment. She testified also that he left a few minutes later, having donned a dark jacket.

---

*He raised his hands and cried, "I am not resisting arrest."*

---

Oswald first waited at the bus stop, which was so close Mrs. Roberts could see him from her window. He waited but a moment and then set off on foot down the street. He was next heard of at the junction of 10th Street and Patton Avenue, almost a mile away, as he approached a policeman who was parked at the roadside after cruising the district in his patrol car. Oswald stooped and conversed with the policeman, Officer J.D. Tippit, through the open window of the car for almost a minute. The officer then got out of the car and, according to the Warren Report account, Lee Harvey Oswald drew his gun and shot him dead before making off in haste. Thirty minutes later, Oswald was seen entering a cinema, the Texas Theatre, without paying and an employee telephoned the police with his description.

The police descended on the Texas Theatre in considerable strength and, when the lights went up, they had no difficulty in finding Oswald in a very sparse audience. He raised his hands and cried, 'I am not resisting arrest,' whereupon he was relieved of a revolver and was taken to Police Headquarters. By shortly before 2 P.M., Dallas Police had arrested the only man who would be accused of the murders of President Kennedy and Officer Tippit.

Two days later, when Lee Harvey Oswald was being transferred from a cell in Police Headquarters to the County Jail, a Dallas citizen, Jack Ruby, stepped out from the crowds of news reporters who were waiting in the basement car park to see the President's killer bundled into a car to make his short journey, and shot him dead in view of all present, plus millions of television viewers.

## The Warren Report

The new President, Lyndon Baines Johnson, ordered an official inquiry into the assassination of President Kennedy, and appointed the Chief Justice of the United States, Earl Warren, to head it. Warren appointed six other people of note and position to his Commission, and with a large staff they began to piece together the events of 22 November 1963. Ten months later the findings of the Presidential Commission were published in a report. The Warren Report, as it became known, occupying 26 volumes and consisting of ten million words, explained that Lee Harvey Oswald, alone and unaided—a lone nut—had shot and killed the President from a sixth-floor window of the Texas School Book Depository, where he worked, and that he had shot and killed Officer J.D. Tippit while on the run. Nightclub owner, Jack Ruby, overcome by grief for his dead President and worried lest the President's widow be subjected to the ordeal of Lee Harvey Oswald's trial, alone and unaided shot and killed Oswald in the basement car park of Dallas Police Headquarters.

Neat, tidy and final. The matter was now settled and the United States—and, indeed, an anxious world—could get on with its business.

---

*The Warren Report advertised distinct one-sidedness.*

---

The reaction of the US media to the Warren Report was certainly interesting. In some respects it was somewhat alarming, also. In the main, American newspapers, radio and television made it quite clear that, as far as they were concerned, the matter was, indeed, settled. The Warren Report had said it all and to challenge the Commission's findings was undesirable—even unpatriotic. Like the government, the public at large and, most certainly, the intelligence agencies, the media had heard exactly what it wanted to hear: there was no conspiracy. It was all the work of a 'lone nut' killer, and the 'lone nut' killer had been killed by another 'lone nut' killer. Weren't they always 'lone nuts' who killed Presidents, anyway? Had they looked a little closer at this conclusion they would have arrived at the more accurate realisation that, once again, a US govern-

ment was arguing the case for a murdered President to have
been the victim of a lone assassin, as they had time and time
again, only to have the lie to this proved by time and seek-
ers after truth.

## Truth Seekers

To the considerable discomfort of the government in general and the Warren Commissioners in particular—and despite the disdain which emanated from the direction of the
media at large—it was not long before there were some who
felt compelled to speak out against the Report and its findings. Lawyer Mark Lane, for instance, was approached by
Marguerite Oswald, Lee's mother, to argue a posthumous
defence for her son. Upon encountering the nitty gritty of
the 26 volumes of the Report, Lane, like other important
researchers such as Sylvia Meagher and Harold Weisberg,
was appalled at the disorder he found. Facts had been distorted and frequently ignored, important witnesses had not
been called and, of those who were, often the accepted and
officially recorded testimony had been dubious. Too often
interrogators had conducted questioning 'off the record' so
that important testimony did not find its way into the pages
of the Report. The Commission had relied solely upon the
FBI to carry out its investigatory work, and the 'Feebies'
submissions to the Commission on many counts left much
to be desired. They were later to be accused of covering
their own backs, for whatever reason. The proceedings of
the Commission were not conducted in a courtroom where
challenge could be made to witnesses' testimony or to the
manner of the proceedings. The Presidential Commission
made no provision for a defence, where that was appropri-
ate, neither, for that matter, for prosecution where that may
have been deemed desirable. In spite of the enormous in-
tegrity loaned to the investigation by Earl Warren and his
colleagues, the Warren Report advertised distinct one-
sidedness. And to cap it all, the Report contained no index,
no means by which researchers could readily unlock the
contents of the daunting 26 volumes. It was Sylvia Meagher
who took upon herself the mountainous task of construct-
ing an index to the Report, its hearings and exhibits, thereby
earning the gratitude of all those who had a need—or a de-
sire—to examine the Report intelligently. She it was who
might claim the accolade for opening the floodgates to the

critics who followed, in profusion, in the wake of the publication of her index in 1966. Her contribution to the research into the assassination of President Kennedy was unique, and her brilliant book *Accessories After the Fact* which was published the following year, demonstrated her incredible grasp of the minute detail of the Report.

Mark Lane, too, made a huge impact with his bestselling book, *Rush to Judgment*, which was also first published in 1966. Though seeking more to establish a defence for Oswald than to probe those areas which might have pointed the direction of those who had committed the crimes for which Oswald had been blamed, he nonetheless contributed in no small way to opening up the Warren Report to the researcher and to the public. Special mention must also be made of Harold Weisberg, who was outstanding for his outspoken, well-informed criticism. His first book, *Whitewash*, was, in fact, so outspoken that he could not find any publisher in the US or Britain to publish it. He replied by publishing it himself. . . .

---

*He replied, "I never killed anybody, no sir."*

---

Any analysis of the works of the Warren Report critics shows that the cry common to them all is that by the means described above—the distortion of testimony, the ignoring of witnesses, the acceptance of unreliable testimony and the biased interpretation of evidence—the Commission had gone out of its way to give credence to testimony and evidence which supported the theory that Lee Harvey Oswald had, alone and unaided, shot and killed the President of the United States, and that they sought to conceal or discredit that which would have opposed it.

The arguments over the assassination of President Kennedy began almost before the sound of the gunfire had died away. How many shots had been fired? Some said two, some said three, four, five and six. From which direction had the shots come? Some said they all came from behind, some said from the front, some said from the front and right of the President. When were the shots fired? Some said when the President's car was in Houston Street, others said when it was in Elm Street. How did Lee Harvey Oswald get away from the Book Depository building? Some said by the front door and by taking a bus and a taxi, while another reliable witness said by the back door, running down Elm Street where he was smartly picked up in a getaway car. The various editions of the Dallas newspapers that day added to the confusion. On the subject of where the President's car was when the shooting occurred, the second edition contradicted the first and the third edition contradicted the second.

## An Eyewitness Speaks

When Lee Harvey Oswald was arrested and taken to Police Headquarters, he was charged at first only with the murder of Officer J.D. Tippit and it was much later that he was charged with the killing of the President. He was filmed, briefly, in an interview with the press when he was asked the question, 'Did you kill the President?' He replied, 'I never killed anybody, no sir.' The reaction of millions of people watching that interview on television must have been, 'What gall! Hadn't they said that eyewitnesses had seen him shoot the President?' In fact there was but one solitary person who claimed to be an eyewitness to Lee Harvey Oswald shooting President Kennedy. His name was Howard Brennan and the acceptance of his testimony provided an example of the kind of thing for which the Warren Commission was most criticised.

Howard L. Brennan sat on a low wall opposite the Texas School Depository building. As the shots were fired he looked up and saw a figure with a rifle at a window on the sixth floor, at the south-east corner. He says he saw the man fire the rifle and pause for a moment as though to make sure he had hit his target before disappearing. Brennan claimed to have given a description of the man he saw at the window to a Secret Service agent named Sorrels, and this is where the problems began. Sorrels had attached himself to the White House detail and he accompanied the President to Parkland Hospital, where massive efforts were made to save him. Anxious to make immediate enquiries, Sorrels made his way back to the Book Depository building, and it was there that Brennan gave him his description of the sniper. Since Sorrels estimated that it took him some 20 to 25 minutes before he arrived back at the Depository, it must have been roughly 1 P.M. when Brennan was speaking to him. Brennan, however, claimed he saw Sorrels within minutes of the shooting, and it is firmly established that a description was broadcast to patrol cars at 12:45 P.M. The Commission never reconciled this discrepancy. Then there was the statement Brennan made in which he claimed the sniper was firing from a standing position. All photographs taken of the window in question at or about the time of the shooting show the window open at the bottom only, so that if Brennan was correct the sniper would have been firing through the glass. The window-sills were fairly low on that floor, and the Commission conceded that '. . . although Brennan testified that the man in the window was standing when he fired the shots, most probably he was either sitting or kneeling'. The Warren Commission thereby contradicted their witness and created another problem. Brennan gave a description which included the height and weight of the sniper and they had now precluded the possibility that Brennan had seen the man standing up; they allowed only that he had seen head and shoulders. The Commission's answer to this was that 'Brennan could have seen enough of the body of a kneeling or squatting person to estimate his height'. The estimation of weight was, no doubt, taken for granted. But of even greater importance was the fact that when Brennan faced Lee Harvey Oswald in a police line-up later on in the same day—and though he had seen Oswald's photograph on television—he did not make a positive identification. In the following months he changed his position again and again, telling FBI men on 17 December 1963 that '. . . he was sure the person firing the rifle was Oswald', and then on 7 January 1964 he '. . . appeared to revert to his earlier inability to make a positive identification'. Four months after the assassination he gave evidence in which he changed his mind yet again, and the record shows that '. . . Howard L. Brennan made a positive identification of Oswald as being the person at the window'. Had all this happened in anything like a normal courtroom Howard L. Brennan's evidence would have been totally and utterly demolished. A curious tailpiece to all this was provided by Dallas Police Chief, Jesse Curry, when he was being interviewed by KRLD-TV. The interviewer asked, 'Chief Curry, do you have an eyewitness who saw someone shoot the President?'

Curry replied, 'No, sir, we do not.'

The interview took place on the morning of 24 November, two days after the President was killed.

## German or Italian?

The Warren Commission sparked off more controversy when it described in detail how Lee Harvey Oswald had, alone and unaided, shot the President twice and Governor John B. Connally, who was sitting in the Lincoln in front of the President, three times. They stated that only three shots had been fired, one of which had missed. Of the two shots which hit, one struck the President only, while the other struck the President, exited his neck, struck Governor Connally, exited his chest only to hit him again in his wrist and to exit once more before finally making a wound in his thigh. Not surprisingly, the bullet purported to have caused all this mayhem was nicknamed by the critics 'The Magic Bullet'. The Warren Commission resolutely clung to this explanation despite Governor Connally's evidence that there was a brief time lag between the President being hit and his own wounding. But then, there was a special and compelling reason for them to do so. The rifle said to be owned by Oswald and which the Commission claimed was the murder weapon, could not have been fired more than three times in the 5.6 seconds in which all the shooting took place. To admit to another shot having been fired would have been to admit the presence of a second sniper, and a second sniper would have indicated that a conspiracy had taken place. The Warren Commission were dedicated to admitting no such thing.

But the day was to yield yet another amazing mystery. During a thorough search of the sixth floor of the School Book Depository a rifle was found. Unhappily for the Warren Commissioners, the four police officers present at the time it was discovered, unanimously identified it as a German 7.65 Mauser. Deputy Sheriff Eugene Boone found the rifle following the movement of book boxes by Deputy Sheriff Luke Mooney and called Deputy Constable Seymour Weitzman to witness his discovery. Another Deputy Sheriff, Roger Craig, was thereabouts and he saw the gun and heard the conversations of the others. The officers had no doubts about their identification and affidavits were drawn up by Boone and Weitzman, who described the weapon in detail, noting the colour of the sling and the scope. Police Captain Will Fritz was also present at the scene and he, also, is claimed to have agreed that the rifle was a 7.65 Mauser. District Attorney Henry M. Wade, in a television interview, referred to the sixth-floor discovery and quoted the weapon as a Mauser, a statement picked up by the press and reported widely. Following the finding of the gun, however, it was collected by Lieutenant J.C. Day and taken to Police Head-quarters, where it was logged as a 6.5 Mannlicher-Carcano, an Italian carbine, bearing the serial number C2766. Mannlicher-Carcano Italian carbine No. C2766, it was claimed, belonged to Lee Harvey Oswald.

---

*They both, nonetheless, changed their testimony and conceded they had made a mistake.*

---

Those concerned with the finding of the rifle at the Book Depository and who had written affidavits, Boone and Weitzman, were pressed, under questioning by the Commission, to review their identification of it. The Mannlicher-Carcano, at first glance, looked very much like [a] 7.65 Mauser, it is true. How would they account, though, for a situation in which they had been close enough to describe the colour of the sling and yet had made an error in identifying the rifle itself? After all, the Mannlicher-Carcano bears the legend 'Made in Italy' on the butt, whereas the German gun has the name 'Mauser' stamped on the barrel! Were these officers unable to read? In spite of any argument which might be brought to bear, they both, nonetheless, changed their testimony and conceded they had made a mistake.

## Consequence of Truth

Young Roger Craig, who saw and heard all that had gone on in the Book Depository, refused to concede that he had been mistaken, or even that he might have been. He was also the key witness to a figure who ran from the back door of the Book Depository down the slope to Elm Street, where he was picked up in a green Rambler station wagon and whisked away. When confronted by Lee Harvey Oswald in the office of Captain Fritz, where he was being questioned, Craig instantly identified him as the man he had seen. His sighting was corroborated by a number of other witnesses, but since a fleeing man picked up by another allowed two people to be conspiring the Warren Commission chose to ignore this evidence. Craig actually identified the driver of the Rambler on a separate occasion when he was present at the questioning of a young man who had been picked up. The young man was released. An attempt was made to discredit Craig by Captain Will Fritz, who asserted that the young deputy had never been present in his office while Oswald was being interrogated. The lie to this was advertised when Police Chief Jesse Curry published his book, *JFK Assassination File*, since a photograph appeared in it clearly showing Craig in Fritz's office and bearing the caption, 'The Homicide Bureau Office under guard while Oswald was being interrogated'.

Roger Craig had been named Officer of the Year by the Dallas Traffic Commission and he was promoted four times. He was to receive no further promotion or commendation after his refusal to withdraw his identification of the Mauser and admit to being wrong about his identification of the man who ran from the Depository to be picked up by the Rambler on Elm Street. For this he suffered the most dire consequences. Craig was forbidden to speak to reporters about these things and when, in 1967, he was caught doing so he was fired. Thereafter he spoke of a consciousness of being followed, and was fired at by an unknown assailant. The bullet came uncomfortably close and, in fact, grazed his head. He began receiving threats and, in 1973, his car was run off a mountain road causing him a back injury, the pain from which was to become a permanent feature of his life. On another occasion his car was bombed. His marriage broke up in 1973 as a consequence of the continuing harassment, which did not abate. In 1975 he was shot at and wounded in the shoulder by another unknown gunman. At the age of 39, Roger Craig, suffering from the stress of the constant back pains he endured and the financial pressures he encountered because of finding it difficult to get work, succumbed, they said, and committed suicide. They said.

# Chapter 2

# The Conspiracy Theories

# 1

# The Mafia Killed
# the President

David E. Scheim

Following a ten-year private investigation, David E. Scheim comes to the shocking conclusion that the Mafia killed President Kennedy. Scheim asserts that Kennedy's anti-crime stance threatened the livelihood of organized crime, which gave the Mob a prime motive to eliminate him. According to Scheim, Jack Ruby shot Lee Harvey Oswald in order to silence him and protect Mafia interests. Ruby, a club owner and member of organized crime, had various underworld contacts that linked him to the assassination. Scheim meticulously studies Ruby's whereabouts and actions days before the president's murder. Scheim believes that Ruby met with other underworld figures from Dallas in preparation for the assassination. Ruby's presence at a Mafia party on November 20 was corroborated by several witnesses. At this function Ruby made contact with Jada, an employee of his and his alibi for a visit to New Orleans; Frank T. Tortoriello, a partner in a Mob-linked construction company; and Joseph Frank Federici, a nephew of a notorious former Mafia boss. On the evening of November 21 Ruby met with a man in a Dallas restaurant. Witnesses describe the man as having a close resemblance to Lee Harvey Oswald. According to Scheim, Ruby's whereabouts and actions before the assassination prove that the Mafia killed the president.

---

Jack Ruby's meetings in New Orleans, New York, Chicago and Miami, four key Mafia bases, were behind him. After a remarkable, 25-fold peak in the first week of November,

David E. Scheim, *Contract on America: The Mafia Murder of President John F. Kennedy*. New York: Shapolsky Publishers, Inc., 1988. Copyright © 1988 by David E. Scheim. Reproduced by permission.

. . . his rate of out-of-state calls plummeted. Now, as November 22 approached, the focus of the Mob activity occupying Ruby shifted to Dallas.

One indication of Ruby's change in pattern during this final period was offered by Nancy Powell, a two-year employee of the Carousel Club. Asked about Ruby's behavior "the couple of weeks or months before President Kennedy was shot," Powell testified:

> He became more relaxed about the club. At first, he would never leave the club. He was there all the time, but he got to where he would go out and come in later like at 10 o'clock or something.

Larry Crafard, who worked full-time at the Carousel Club for one month in November 1963, was more specific. Crafard told the FBI that during November, Ruby would typically spend one or two hours in the early afternoon at the club. He would then leave for the day, return at about 10 P.M., and remain there until closing at about 1:30 or 2 A.M.

Crafard amplified when subsequently questioned by Warren Commission counsel:

> Q: So as I understand it . . . he would spend 8 or 10 [of] what would presumably be waking hours away from the club each day.
>
> Mr. Crafard: Yes.
>
> Q: Did he ever talk about what he was doing during that period of time?
>
> Mr. Crafard: No.
>
> Q: Did you ever hear anything or do you have any idea of what he was doing during that period of time?
>
> Mr. Crafard: No.

Crafard also testified that during November 1963, "people would come to the club to see him, he would go downstairs, leave with them, and sometimes would be gone the rest of the afternoon."

By mid-November, however, Ruby no longer had time for routine Carousel-based racketeering; he no longer had any reason for placing calls from his night club office to Mobsters across the country. Now, as documented in National Archives files, Ruby was busy receiving Mob guests from out of town, meeting with other underworld figures from Dallas, and assisting in the final preparations for President Kennedy's murder. . . .

## A Mafia Party

Following the usual pattern, Ruby and two associates related conflicting innocuous activities to explain his whereabouts on the night of November 20. This time, however, the cover was penetrated by detailed independent reports.

Beginning in the late evening of November 20, Frank T. Tortoriello held an all-night party at his residence in the Tanglewood Apartments in Dallas. According to the FBI's first report of this party, Tortoriello's guests were Jada, the Carousel stripper, Jack Ruby, Joe F. Frederici, plus Frederici's wife, Sandy, and Tortoriello's next-door neighbor, Ann Bryant. Subsequent FBI reports provided more information about the party and about the intriguing relationships of three of those present.

Frank T. Tortoriello, the host, was a partner in a Mob-linked construction company and a buddy of Mafioso Joseph Campisi. Another friend of Tortoriello was Jada, the Carousel stripper, who spent several nights in his apartment during and before November 1963.

---

*Ruby was busy receiving Mob guests from out of town.*

---

Joseph Frank Federici, aliases Frederici, Frederica and Frederico, was described to the FBI as a nephew of Vito Genovese, the notorious former Mafia boss from New Jersey. Federici's background was consistent with that relationship. For one thing, he was a New Jersey resident who lived in Dallas, at the Tanglewood Apartments, only between February 1963 and January 1964. During that period, another Tanglewood resident reported, he was "allegedly employed in the management consultant business at Dallas for his father, who allegedly resides in Trenton, New Jersey.". . .

The most striking clue to Ruby's presence at Tortoriello's party, however, was his association with the others present. Jada, of course, was Ruby's employee and the alibi for his June visit to New Orleans. Tortoriello was a close associate of Ruby, as Tortoriello told the FBI. Finally, Federici's name was found among Ruby's personal effects, and Federici confirmed his acquaintance with Ruby.

Whatever the nature of Tortoriello's party—strictly a social function, a break from organization business, or a pre-assassination gala—it was another timely Mafia contact of Ruby covered by a suspicious maze of contradictory accounts. Timely, too, was Federici's departure from Dallas to Providence, Rhode Island "during the early morning of November 22, 1963." Federici explained that he left Dallas with his wife "to visit relatives."

## A Suspicious Office Visit

About 10:30 or 11 A.M. on Thursday, November 21, Ruby told the FBI, he drove a young friend, Connie Trammel, to the office of Lamar Hunt. According to Trammel, who supported Ruby's account, she went to see Hunt, a son of oil tycoon H.L. Hunt, for an employment interview. After dropping Trammel off, Ruby related, he met with one of two attorneys—he couldn't remember which one—in the building in which Lamar Hunt's office was located. Ruby then waited around in the lobby for Trammel to come down, he reported, and finally left the building. A more direct contact with Lamar Hunt, however, is indicated in the February 24, 1964 memo of Warren Commission counsel Hubert and Griffin: "Ruby visited his office on November 21. Hunt denies knowing Ruby. Ruby gives innocent explanation."

The reported contact between Ruby and Lamar Hunt is consistent with the appearance of the name "Lamar Hunt" in one of Ruby's notebooks and Ruby's acquaintance with Lamar's father, H.L. Hunt. And it raises suspicion in view of the Hunts' sharp antagonism toward President Kennedy. During a party before the fateful Dallas visit . . . H.L. reportedly remarked that there was "no way left to get those traitors out of government except by shooting them out," referring to President Kennedy. Also, H.L.'s son Nelson Bunker Hunt co-sponsored the black-bordered ad attacking President Kennedy that appeared in the *Dallas Morning News* on November 22. . . .

## Stalking Kennedy in Houston

On December 4, 1963, Secret Service agent Elmer Moore questioned Ruby "regarding his whereabouts and movements" on Thursday, November 21. Ruby reported visiting the Merchants State Bank downtown; according to Connie Trammel, he stopped in on the way to Lamar Hunt's office. As for Ruby's activities that afternoon, however, the usual contradictions plagued his alibi.

The only other thing that Ruby could recall about his activities Thursday was that he "talked to a bartender named Mickey Ryan" at the Carousel Club, "probably in the early afternoon hours." Andrew Armstrong, the Carousel's handyman, also reported that Ruby was at the club Thursday afternoon "with Mickey Ryan, a bartender who wanted to borrow money from Ruby." But Ryan told the FBI he did not recall meeting Ruby at the Carousel Club that day. In fact, Ryan believed that he "last saw Ruby approximately two weeks prior to November 22." In further support of Ruby's alibi, Andrew Armstrong reported that he believed Ruby called some American Guild of Variety Artists (AGVA) officials from the Carousel Club Thursday afternoon "regarding auditions of amateurs." But telephone records show no calls from the Carousel Club that day.

---

*It was another timely Mafia contact of Ruby covered by a suspicious maze of contradictory accounts.*

---

What was Ruby actually doing Thursday afternoon? His telephone records provide a further clue. Mrs. Billy Chester Carr, a Houston booking agent, told the FBI that Ruby called her on November 19, and again on November 21 between 2:30 and 3 P.M. Ruby's toll call records show the reported call to Carr in Houston on November 19 but no such call on November 21. By Thursday afternoon, however, Ruby did not have to place a toll call to reach Houston. For Ruby was there, monitoring President Kennedy's movements in preparation for the next day's assassination in Dallas.

On December 2, 1963, Secret Service agent Lane Bertram filed a detailed report of a three-day investigation conducted in Houston. It opened with this synopsis:

> Numerous witnesses identify Jack Leon Rubenstein [also known as] Jack Ruby, as being in Houston, Texas on November 21, for several hours, one block from

the President's entrance route and from the Rice Hotel where he stayed.

On November 26, as his report describes, Special Agent Bertram interviewed five witnesses who saw Ruby on the 400 block of Milam Street in Houston Thursday afternoon. One was a Houston deputy sheriff, Bill Williams, who "saw the man on two or three different occasions and talked to him about 3 P.M." Williams "was sure the picture of Ruby appearing in the paper was identical with the man he observed." After conducting these interviews, Bertram secured police photographs of Ruby and presented them to the five witnesses. "All agree[d] that in their opinion Jack Rubenstein was in Houston on November 21 from about 2:30 to 7:15 P.M., in close proximity to the President's route to the hotel and the Rice Hotel itself."

---

*Ruby was there, monitoring President Kennedy's movements.*

---

It is noteworthy that Ruby was first sighted in Houston at about 2:30 to 3 P.M., the same time that Carr received a call from him. This is also the time at which he would have arrived in Houston if he had left Dallas at about noon and driven the 243 miles on the freeway to Houston at an 80- to 100-mile-per-hour Texas clip. Such a speed would have been natural for Ruby given his many traffic violations, including four for speeding. . . .

Ruby's interest in President Kennedy's movements was explicitly reported by one witness, Gloria Reece. Reece stated that

> the subject asked her if she was going to the "President's dinner." She advised him that she had not been invited and asked him to buy her a beer and attempted to make a date with him. The subject declined, stating that he was in a hurry and departed going in the direction of the Coliseum where the President was to appear at the Albert Thomas Appreciation Dinner.

It is therefore difficult to dispute Special Agent Bertram's conclusion that Ruby's visit "very probably had some connection with the President's appearance in Houston.". . .

## Three Assassination-Eve Contacts

At about 10 P.M., as reported by several sources, Ruby stopped in for about 45 minutes at the Egyptian Lounge, a Dallas underworld hangout. One of its owners was Joseph Campisi, a top-ranking Dallas Mafioso close to Carlos Marcello and Marcello's Mafia-involved brothers. When questioned by the House Assassinations Committee in 1978, Campisi said that he was not at the Egyptian Lounge on the night of November 21 and had not known Ruby was there. But on December 7, 1963, Campisi had told the FBI of his "contact with Ruby" that Thursday night, "when Ruby came to the Egyptian Lounge for a steak."

About midnight, Ruby stopped in at a restaurant in the Teamster-financed Dallas Cabana Hotel. With Ruby was Larry Meyers, who had checked into the Cabana that day, as had Mobster Eugene Brading. A sales executive for a Chicago sporting goods firm, Meyers smoothly explained this contact with Ruby as a social encounter and cited specific business engagements to justify his presence in Dallas. Yet there are hints of suspicion about Meyers and this rendezvous with Ruby. . . .

During interrogation by Warren Commission counsel, the mention of Meyers' name prompted a blank pause from Ruby's associate Ralph Paul and a tirade about Ruby's racketeering acquaintances from his sister Eva, who denied knowing Meyers. And in different interviews, Meyers presented detailed but totally contradictory accounts of subsequent contact with Ruby on November 23. Meyers' accounts of activities Friday afternoon and Sunday morning were also inconsistent.

---

*Ruby's visit "very probably had some connection with the President's appearance in Houston."*

---

Following his encounters with Joseph Campisi at the Egyptian Lounge and with Larry Meyers at the Cabana, Ruby met a third man at a third Dallas restaurant. At about 1:30 A.M. Friday, a young man walked into the Lucas B&B Restaurant and sat down at a table. About an hour later, as recounted by B&B waitress Mary Lawrence, "Jack Ruby came into the B&B Restaurant and, after looking at the young man at the table, sat down at a table behind the cash register. He did not order his usual food, stating he didn't feel good, and ordered a large glass of orange juice. A few minutes later, the young man who was seated at the table went over to Ruby's table. Thereafter Ruby paid the bill for both himself and the young man who had eaten."

After President Kennedy was shot and Oswald arrested later that day, Lawrence was struck by a close resemblance between the man with Ruby and photographs of Oswald. She told the FBI that both she and the night shift cashier "agreed that he appeared very similar to Lee Harvey Oswald." She further reported that the man was "in his 20's, 5'7"–9", medium build, 140 lbs.," with "dark hair." This exactly matched Oswald's characteristics: 24 years old, 5'9", 140 lbs., with brown hair. Later in her FBI interview, however, Lawrence added one detail that seemed to preclude this man being Oswald—he had "a small scar near his mouth, either on the right or left side."

---

*Lawrence was struck by a close resemblance between the man with Ruby and photographs of Oswald.*

---

When subsequently questioned by the Dallas Police, Lawrence provided a virtually identical account of the assassination morning encounter, and stated that the man with Ruby "was positively Lee Harvey Oswald." Later in that interview, however, she backed down from her positive identification and once more reported a scar on Ruby's visitor. Yet her initial positive identification is credible given other accounts of prior encounters between Ruby and Oswald at the Carousel Club, testimony by Ruby calling attention to that possibility and contradictory reports by Ruby and an associate about his whereabouts early November 22. It is also pertinent to note that on December 3, 1963, two days before her FBI interview, as she reported, an unknown male had called Lawrence and told her, "If you don't want to die, you better get out of town."

## Drinks at the "Cellar Door"

Meanwhile, during the early Friday morning hours, ten Secret Service agents enjoyed liquid refreshments at the Cellar Door night club in Fort Worth. As disclosed in a Secret

Service report, among those present were five of the eight agents who would ride in the car directly behind President Kennedy's, plus two other members of the White House detail. Most stayed until at least 2:45 A.M., and one stayed until 5:00 A.M., although many had to report for duty by 8:00 that morning.

---

*Ruby observed the critical event of that day from a perfect vantage point.*

---

The agents went to the Cellar Door that night on the specific invitation of its owner, Pat Kirkwood. Kirkwood provided them drinks on the house, but he and his manager assured the Secret Service in subsequent interviews that these drinks were all non-alcoholic and that no alcoholic drinks were served in their club. In 1978, however, Kirkwood volunteered to the *Dallas Morning News* that he would keep "several bottles of liquor reserved for special customers, like doctors, lawyers or off-duty policemen—people I figured I might have to depend upon later in life.". . .

The purpose of Kirkwood's hospitality to President Kennedy's Secret Service guards was suggested in the testimony of another Carousel stripper, Nancy Powell. After several hours of questioning, Powell mentioned Kirkwood's Cellar Door night club, "where the Secret Service men go." She then threw out this comment: "Pat said he would probably be called to ask him about *getting them drunk on purpose*."

## A Ringside View

Between 9:00 and 9:30 A.M. on November 22, Dallas Police Officer T.M. Hansen, Jr. saw Jack Ruby outside the Dallas Police building. Hansen told the FBI that Ruby was standing with four or five others "directly to the side of the stairway which leads to the basement" at the Harwood Street entrance. As Hansen passed Ruby, whom he knew casually, Hansen "shook his hand and said good morning."

Filling in Ruby's alibi for later that morning was Tony Zoppi, the entertainment columnist who lamented reports of "quick buck artists" linking Ruby to the Mob and the assassination. At about 10:30 A.M. Friday morning, according to Zoppi and Ruby, Ruby stopped in at Zoppi's office in the Dallas Morning News building. Zoppi said that Ruby had come to discuss "an ESP expert he wanted Zoppi to plug"; Ruby testified that he picked up a brochure about a memory expert while in Zoppi's office that morning.

. . . However, this story was fatally flawed. For in a 1978 Congressional interview, Zoppi detailed his assassination morning conversation with Ruby; Zoppi noted that Ruby appeared "too calm that morning to have been involved in a conspiracy." Ruby's script of events, however, included no actual meeting with Zoppi. Ruby told the FBI in 1963 that a few hours before the assassination, he "went to the office of Tony Zoppi, but Tony was not there." Ruby subsequently testified that he "went down there Friday morning to Tony Zoppi's office, and they said he went to New Orleans for a couple of days."

Ruby related that he remained in the Dallas Morning News building all morning to place his regular weekend ads for his night clubs. Even after the noon deadline for the ads had passed, Ruby hung around another half hour, although President Kennedy's motorcade was to drive by just a few blocks away. It was especially curious that Ruby missed the chance to see his professed "idol," since two "partial" Wednesday newspapers showing the motorcade route were found in Ruby's car. During his polygraph hearing of July 1964, Ruby himself noted this problem in his story:

> Oh yes; they didn't ask me another question: "if I loved the President so much, why wasn't I at the parade?"

But in fact, Ruby observed the critical event of that day from a perfect vantage point. An FBI chronology summarized,

> Ruby was on the second floor, front of the Dallas Morning News Building which looks out at the TSBD [Texas School Book Depository] Building. At about the time the President was shot, Ruby allegedly would have a perfect view of the front of the TSBD Building. . . .

> [Ruby was] allegedly sitting in the only chair from which he could observe the site of the President's assassination. . . .

> Georgia Mayor, secretary in the Advertising Division, Dallas Morning News, advised that when she returned from lunch at approximately 12:30 P.M., Jack Ruby was

sitting in a chair directly in front of her desk. She believes that Ruby had been looking out at the scene when the President was shot. . . .

## Lethal Finale

At 12:30 P.M., as Ruby anxiously watched, a shot was fired at President Kennedy from the Texas School Book Depository; it inflicted a minor, shallow wound in Kennedy's shoulder. In the limousine of Vice President Johnson, Secret Service Agent Rufus Youngblood reacted instantly; Johnson reported that Youngblood "turned in a flash, immediately after the first explosion, hitting me on the shoulder, and shouted to all of us in the back seat to get down." During the next eight seconds, however, not even a warning was shouted from the agents in President Kennedy's follow-up car—five of whom had been so solicitously hosted early that morning at Kirkwood's Cellar Door. And then, a bullet was fired from behind the stockade fence in the grassy knoll; President Kennedy's skull splintered backward.

---

*Ruby fired the shot that ensured Oswald's everlasting silence.*

---

Soon afterward, a man who identified himself as Jim Braden was arrested in the Dal-Tex Building opposite Dealey Plaza. According to police reports, Braden was in the building "without a good excuse" when President Kennedy was assassinated. Six years later, a trace of Braden's driver's license revealed that he was actually Eugene Hale Brading, a prominent California Mobster with 35 arrests and three convictions under six aliases. Questioned then by Los Angeles Police, Brading provided a highly dubious alibi for his whereabouts at the time of the assassination.

Dallas Mafioso Joseph Campisi reported that he was driving his car when he heard about the assassination, but could not remember where. Campisi also had trouble remembering whether he had met with Ruby the night before, but police records confirmed that he did meet with Ruby in jail on November 30.

At 1:30 P.M., an hour after viewing Kennedy's shooting from his prime vantage point, Ruby dropped by Parkland

Hospital to ascertain its outcome. At about the same time, in the Oak Cliff section of Dallas, Police Officer J.D. Tippit, a close associate of Ruby, was shot to death. During the next two days . . . Ruby met with another Dallas Police crony, Harry Olsen, and repeatedly visited the police building, where Lee Harvey Oswald was being held. At 11:17 A.M. Sunday morning, as others established an elaborate alibi for him and coordinated the split-second timing, Ruby left the downtown Western Union office to pay another such visit. And at 11:21 A.M., in the crowning action of his Mob career, Ruby fired the shot that ensured Oswald's everlasting silence.

## Witnesses Drop Like Flies

Following a classic pattern, many others with potentially incriminating information were subsequently murdered or intimidated. Representative was the fate of Karen Carlin, who Ruby hinted was "part of the conspiracy." In a Secret Service interview the evening of Oswald's murder, hysterical with terror, Carlin stated that she was "under the impression that Lee Harvey Oswald, Jack Ruby and other individuals unknown to her, were involved in a plot to assassinate President Kennedy." She feared that "she would be killed if she gave any information to authorities" and asked that "all information she had related be kept confidential to prevent retaliation." Carlin also testified that after the president was shot, Cellar Door owner Pat Kirkwood called and told her, "I want you down here in about 20 minutes." When she refused, Kirkwood told her, "If you're not down here, you won't be around too long." Several months later, she was found shot to death in a Houston hotel.

Yet some witnesses survived to present highly incriminating testimony. Three informants detailed assassination designs against the Kennedys that were expressed in 1962 by New Orleans Mafia boss Carlos Marcello, Tampa chieftain Santos Trafficante and their Teamster ally, Jimmy Hoffa. Johnny Roselli, whose body was found floating in an oil drum after testifying in secret session before the Senate Intelligence Committee, reported that Jack Ruby was "one of our boys" and had been ordered to murder Oswald to silence him. Crucial, too, was the testimony of this tormented conspirator, who had come to face the same sinister pressure for silence. On June 7, 1964, stating that he could not tell the truth in Dallas and repeatedly expressing fears for his life, Jack Ruby pleaded with Chief Justice Earl Warren for a hearing in Washington. Although Warren inexplicably refused, Ruby was able to slip in many candid disclosures during his testimony in Dallas.

Ruby mocked his canned alibi ("I must be a great actor") and indicated conspiracy in the Oswald murder ("If it were timed that way, then, someone in the police department is guilty of giving the information as to when Lee Harvey Oswald was coming down"). He repeatedly called attention to his underworld connections, his opportunity for contacts with Oswald and Tippit, his "numerous phone calls, long-distance calls, all over the country." And it was clearly his own confession, not another's accusation, when he said, "Maybe I was put here as a front of the underworld and sooner or later they will get something out of me that they want done to their advantage.". . .

And so, when the evidence is sorted and arranged, the pieces of the assassination puzzle fall neatly into place. Gracing the tableau are neither crackpots nor clowns, freak coincidences nor senseless crimes. Rather, coming sharply into focus is the vicious combine of killers suspected by Europeans from the start, a group with the motive and capability to perform the assassination. Indeed, the conclusion is clear: the Mafia killed President Kennedy.

# 2

# The FBI Perpetrated a Cover-Up

Peter Dale Scott

Peter Dale Scott, a former Canadian diplomat and professor of English at the University of California, Berkeley, is a poet, writer, and researcher. Scott's research on the assassination of John F. Kennedy led him to believe that the FBI strongly influenced the Warren Commission. The FBI did not want the Warren Commission to come to any other conclusion than the "lone-assassin" theory that the bureau itself had promulgated. The Warren Commission planned to hire its own investigative staff; however, through various manipulations by the FBI, the commission found itself entirely dependent on the bureau for facts. Scott unfolds a conspiratorial cover-up in which the FBI distorted and omitted information during the investigation to protect major governmental interests. For instance, the FBI hid Jack Ruby's connection to organized crime by failing to forward certain documents to the Warren Commission. Scott also examines how the bureau dismissed pertinent information from an informant who had taped an interview with a white racist. That person told the informant that members of Congress were involved in planning the president's assassination, but the FBI claimed the information could not be verified and conveniently never told the Warren Commission about the tape.

For its part, the FBI undoubtedly tried to ensure that the Warren Commission would reach the . . . conclusion [that one man, acting alone, killed the president]. [J. Edgar]

Peter Dale Scott, *Deep Politics and the Death of JFK.* Berkeley: University of California Press, 1993. Copyright © 1993 by The Regents of the University of California. Reproduced by permission.

Hoover even intervened at the *Washington Post* to block a proposed editorial calling for the establishment of . . . a presidential commission [a special investigative body]; he claimed that, given the FBI's "intensive investigation," a further review would "muddy waters."

Later, when Commission member Allen Dulles warned his old CIA colleague James Angleton that the Warren Commission was considering hiring its own investigative staff, Angleton passed the warning along to the FBI. FBI Deputy Associate Director Alan H. Belmont noted that the Commission "should be discouraged from having an investigative staff" and as a first step moved to limit the number of copies of the first secret FBI report made available to the Commission.

---

*This dependence [on the FBI] made it virtually impossible for the Commission to check out independently published allegations.*

---

Thus it was by no accident, but Justice Department policy, that the Warren Commission found itself dependent for facts on the FBI, which had already (as Commission counsel J. Lee Rankin complained in January 1964) "decided that it is [Lee Harvey] Oswald who committed the assassination" and that "no one else was involved."

This dependence [on the FBI] made it virtually impossible for the Commission to check out independently published allegations—backed by a hearsay report that the name and phone number of FBI Agent James Hosty were in Oswald's address book—that Oswald was an FBI informant. The FBI, when it learned of the Commission's interest in Oswald's pre-assassination FBI contacts, did belatedly confirm this report. Earlier, however, the FBI had provided a typewritten transcription of Oswald's address book in which the Hosty entry was omitted: the relevant page of this transcript was actually retyped, and its contents then failed to fill the page by just the number of lines of the missing Hosty entry. The House Committee confirmed that the Hosty entry had been deleted in the retyping of the memo. It called this incident "regrettable," but "trivial," even though what was at stake was an apparently false statement by FBI officials under oath.

## Jack Ruby and Organized Crime

FBI documents released in 1979 show other instances in which key information was either altered before it reached the Warren Commission, or else withheld altogether. For example, judging from Warren Commission records, the FBI covered up Jack Ruby's connections to organized crime. The Commission did not receive an important interview with Luis Kutner, a Chicago lawyer who had just told the press (correctly) about Ruby's connections to Chicago mobsters Lennie Patrick and Dave Yaras. All the FBI transmitted was a meaningless follow-up interview in which Kutner merely said he had no additional information.

Apparently the FBI also failed to transmit a teletype revealing that Yaras, a national hit man for the Chicago syndicate who had grown up with Ruby, and who had been telephoned by one of Ruby's Teamster contacts on the eve of the assassination, was about to attend a "hoodlum meeting" of top East and West Coast syndicate representatives, including some from the "family" of the former Havana crime lord Santos Trafficante.

---

*The Warren Commission never heard about the alleged Ruby-"Santos" contact.*

---

It is therefore significant that the FBI also suppressed a report that a British freelance newsman, John Wilson-Hudson, claimed to have been in a Havana prison in 1959 with "an American gangster named Santos" (presumably Trafficante), when "Santos" was visited by someone called Ruby whom the newsman believed was Jack Ruby. Wilson-Hudson had offered to look at photographs of Jack Ruby to see if he was indeed that visitor, but FBI headquarters, in an urgent cable to London, vetoed the suggestion: "Prior information available at Bureau that Ruby in Havana, Cuba, in 1959. Bureau desires no further investigation re Wilson." In this way the Warren Commission never heard about the alleged Ruby-"Santos" contact. Nor did it see allegations in the FBI files that linked Ruby at that time to Trafficante's Miami associate Dave Yaras "through shylocking and girls." (The House Committee report, while also ignoring the Yaras allegation, found the Ruby-Trafficante meeting "a distinct possibility.")

Such blatant interference by FBI headquarters in the investigative process is recorded in the files only rarely. But this only confirms that the bureau's professed lack of interest in a lead to "Santos" probably derived not from ignorance but from knowledge—perhaps knowledge of the CIA's use of Trafficante and Chicago crime boss Sam Giancana in plots to assassinate [Cuban premier] Fidel Castro, since CIA embarrassment about this relationship had already led the Justice Department to drop criminal charges in another case involving Giancana. That would be a relatively nonconspiratorial explanation for the bureau's intervention—an example of "induced cover-up" through appeals to "national security."

## The FBI's Cover-Up of a Prior Warning

Such an explanation is less plausible for the FBI's interference with leads that appeared to be guiding its agents to the actual assassins of the President—a case, seemingly, of obstruction of justice, or worse. How else should one assess the response of FBI headquarters to a report from Miami that Joseph Adams Milteer, a white racist with Klan connections, had in early November 1963 correctly warned that a plot to kill the President "from an office building with a high-powered rifle" was already "in the working"? These words are taken from a tape-recording of a discussion between Milteer and his friend, Miami police informant Bill Somersett. Miami police provided copies of this tape to both the Secret Service and the FBI on November 10, 1963, two weeks before the assassination, and this led to the cancellation of a planned motorcade for the President in Miami on November 18.

---

*"I guess you thought I was kidding you when I said he would be killed from a window with a high-powered rifle."*

---

Although an extremist, Milteer was no loner. Southern racists were well organized in 1963, in response to federal orders for desegregation; and Milteer was an organizer for two racist parties, the National States Rights party and the Constitution party. In addition he had attended an April 1963 meeting in New Orleans of the Congress of Freedom, Inc., which had been monitored by an informant for the Miami police. A Miami detective's report of the Congress included the statement that "there was indicated the overthrow of the present government of the United States," including "the setting up of a criminal activity to assassinate particular persons." The report added that "membership within the Congress of Freedom, Inc., contain high ranking members of the armed forces that secretly belong to the organization."

---

*The crime was plotted in such a way that to unravel it would threaten major governmental interests.*

---

In other words, the deep politics of racist intrigue had become intermingled, in the Congress as elsewhere, with the resentment within the armed forces against their civilian commander. Perhaps the most important example in 1963 was that of General Edwin Walker, whom Oswald was accused of stalking and shooting at. Forced to retire in 1962 for disseminating right-wing propaganda in the armed forces, Walker was subsequently arrested at the "Ole Miss" anti-desegregation riots. Nor was the FBI itself exempt from racist intrigue: Milteer, on tape, reported detailed plans for the murder of Martin Luther King, Jr., whom Hoover's FBI, by the end of 1963, had also targeted for (in their words) "neutralizing . . . as an effective Negro leader."

## Denial

Four days after the assassination Somersett reported that Milteer had been "jubilant" about it: "Everything ran true to form. I guess you thought I was kidding you when I said he would be killed from a window with a high-powered rifle." Milteer also was adamant that he had not been "guessing" in his original prediction. In both of the relevant FBI reports from Miami, Somersett was described as "a source who had furnished reliable information in the past."

What was the response of FBI headquarters to the second report? An order was sent to Miami to "amend the reliability statement to show that some of the information furnished by [Somersett] is such that it could not be verified or corroborated." The headquarters file copy noted that "investigation by Atlanta has indicated there is no truth in the statements by [Somersett] and that Milteer was in Quitman, Georgia, during perti[n]ent period."

This notation referred to an interview by the Atlanta FBI with Milteer himself, who quite understandably denied ever having threatened Kennedy, or even having "heard anyone make such threats." This simple denial was forwarded to the Warren Commission in December 1963; but the reports from Somersett (duly rewritten to make them less credible) were not forwarded until August 7, 1964, when the Commission had almost completed its work. Nothing was ever said to the Commission about the tape in the FBI's possession that proved conclusively that Somersett had reported his conversation truthfully, and that Milteer, in his denial, was lying. Nor did the Commission hear about this tape from the Secret Service.

## More Manipulation

In their cover-up of the Milteer tape, the FBI and the Secret Service concealed the fact that they had both had prior warning of "plans . . . to kill President John F. Kennedy." But Milteer had predicted, correctly, not merely the modus operandi of the assassination but also the cover-up:

> SOMERSETT: Boy, if that Kennedy gets shot, we have got to know where we are at. Because you know that will be a real shake, if they do that.

> MILTEER: They wouldn't leave any stone unturned there no way. They will pick up somebody within hours afterwards, if anything like that would happen, just to throw the public off.

Since 1963 both Milteer, the extremist, and Somersett, the informant, have died. Their deaths might seem to corroborate the *Washington Post*'s opinion in 1978 that it was by then too late to pursue the "cold trails" of the John F. Kennedy assassination. But the important leads here pertain not so much to the crime as to the cover-up, not so much to events in Miami or in Dallas as to those inside the FBI and other government agencies. For example, following the analogy of Watergate, one candidate it might be useful to interrogate is Robert P. Gemberling, a retired special agent under whose supervision the page with the missing Hosty entry was retyped, and through whose hands the important

Somersett interviews reached the Warren Commission nine months late. It is not likely that Gemberling, an apparently modest and mild-mannered man, has important knowledge bearing directly on the assassination; but . . . he could perhaps lead interviewers to those involved at a higher level in conspiratorial cover-up.

## Motives Behind the Cover-Up

The existence of a cover-up does not prove that the U.S. government itself was somehow involved in the crime. It does however suggest that the crime was plotted in such a way that to unravel it would threaten major governmental interests, thus inducing a cover-up. The stakes might have been world peace, if a foreign power was, or falsely appeared to be, implicated; or a sensitive government operation, with which Oswald may well have been connected, whether or not he was involved in the actual killing.

Neither of these examples is hypothetical. Within hours of the assassination, officials in Dallas and elsewhere were suggesting, on the flimsiest of evidence, that Oswald was part of a Communist conspiracy, acting on orders out of Havana or Moscow. Worse yet, highly dubious reports, already in U.S. intelligence files, provided some backing for these false conspiracy stories—which soon began to circulate about Jack Ruby as well. Thus, in the context of rumors that were as dangerous as they were misleading, reasonable men may well have settled on a "lone assassin" hypothesis for pragmatic reasons, as less misleading and less dangerous than the alternative theories already circulating. One need not, therefore, assume malevolent motives on the part of all those who engaged in the cover-up.

The motives of Hoover and the FBI cannot be so rationalized. On the Milteer matter alone, they clearly intervened to prevent the examination of legitimate leads. They helped invent misleading biographies of both Ruby and Oswald as "loners," in such a way as to ignore, and thus protect, the almost certain involvement of organized crime.

# 3

# A Team of Assassins Killed Kennedy

Jim Garrison, interviewed by *Playboy*

In a candid interview in July 1967, *Playboy* magazine gave New Orleans District Attorney Jim Garrison the opportunity to rebut charges made against him concerning his investigation of President Kennedy's death. Through his investigations, Garrison concluded that Kennedy was murdered by a group of seven men, including anti-Castro Cuban exiles and members of the paramilitary right. The anti-Castro contingency faulted Kennedy for his lack of support during their attempt to overthrow the regime of Communist Fidel Castro. Following the assassination, nitrate tests were done on Oswald to determine if he had recently fired a rifle. Garrison claims that the absence of nitrate on Oswald's cheeks proves he could not have shot Kennedy. Garrison also observes that two-thirds of the witnesses from Dealey Plaza stated that they heard shots come from the grassy knoll area, invalidating the Warren Report's "lone-assassin" theory. Finally, he supports his conspiracy theory by describing the sequence of shots that took place at the assassination.

---

*Playboy: Even if Lee Harvey Oswald was a scapegoat in the alleged conspiracy, why do you believe he couldn't also have been one of those who shot at the President?*

*[Jim] Garrison:* If there's one thing the Warren Commission and its 26 volumes of supportive evidence demonstrate conclusively, it's that Lee Harvey Oswald did not shoot John Kennedy on November 22, 1963. Of course, the Commis-

sion concluded not only that Oswald fired at the President but that he was a marksman, that he had enough time to "fire three shots, with two hits, within 4.8 and 5.6 seconds," that his Mannlicher-Carcano was an accurate rifle, etc.—but all these conclusions are actually in direct contradiction of the evidence within the Commission's own 26 volumes. By culling and coordinating that evidence, the leading critics of the Commission have proved that Oswald was a mediocre shot; that the Mannlicher-Carcano rifle he allegedly used was about the crummiest weapon on the market today; that its telescopic sight was loose and had to be realigned before Commission experts could fire it; that the 20-year-old ammunition he would have had to use could not have been relied on to fire accurately, if at all; that the rifle quite possibly was taken from Oswald's home after the assassination and planted in the [Texas School Book] Depository; that the Commission's own chronology of Oswald's movements made it highly implausible for him to fire three shots, wipe the rifle clear of fingerprints—there were none found on it—hide the rifle under a stack of books and rush down four flights of stairs to the second floor, all in the few seconds it took Roy Truly and Officer Marrion Baker to rush in from the street after the shots and encounter Oswald standing beside the vending machine in the employees' cafeteria. . . .

## The Nitrate Test

The nitrate test administered to Oswald on the day of the assassination clearly exonerated him of having fired a rifle within the past 24 hours. He had nitrates on both hands, but no nitrates on his cheek—which means it was impossible for him to have fired a rifle. The fact that he had nitrates on both hands is regarded in the nitrate test as a sign of innocence; it's the same as having nitrates on neither hand. This is because so many ordinary objects leave traces of nitrate on the hands. You're smoking a cigar, for example—tobacco contains nitrate; so if you were tested right now, you'd have nitrate on your right hand but not on your left. I'm smoking a pipe, which I interchange between my hands, so I'll have traces of nitrate on both hands but not on my cheeks. The morning of the assassination, Oswald was moving crates in a newly painted room, which was likely to have left traces of nitrate on both his hands. Now, of course, if the nitrate test had proved positive, and Oswald did have nitrate on one hand and on his cheek, that would still not constitute proof positive that he'd fired a gun, because the nitrates could have been left by a substance other than gunpowder. But the fact that he had no nitrate whatsoever on his cheek is ineluctable proof that he never fired a rifle that day. . . .

An expert was dug up who testified that in a Mannlicher-Carcano rifle, the chamber is so tight that no nitrates are emitted upon firing; and the Commission used this testimony to dismiss the whole subject. However, the inventor of the nitrate test subsequently tested the Mannlicher-Carcano and found that it did leave nitrate traces. He was not called to testify by the Warren Commission. So the nitrate test alone is incontrovertible proof that Oswald did not fire a rifle on November 22nd. We've also found some new evidence that shows that Oswald's Mannlicher-Carcano was not the only weapon discovered in the Depository Building after the assassination. I recently traveled to New York for a conference with Richard Sprague, a brilliant man who's been independently researching technical aspects of the assassination, and he showed me a hitherto unpublicized collection of film clips from a motion picture taken of the assassination and its aftermath. Part of the film, shot shortly after one P.M., shows the Dallas police carrying the assassination weapon out of the Book Depository. They stop for the photographers and an officer holds the rifle up above his head so that the inquisitive crowd can look at it. There's just one little flaw here: This rifle does not have a telescopic sight, and thus cannot be Oswald's rifle. This weapon was taken from the building approximately 20 minutes before Oswald's Mannlicher-Carcano was "discovered"—or planted—on the premises. To sum up: Oswald was involved in the conspiracy; shots were fired at Kennedy from the Depository but also from the grassy knoll and apparently from the Dal-Tex Building as well—but not one of them was fired by Lee Harvey Oswald, and not one of them from his Mannlicher-Carcano.

## Assassins on the Grassy Knoll

*Playboy: If Oswald didn't shoot President Kennedy from the sixth-floor window of the Book Depository, who did?*
*Garrison:* Our office has developed evidence that the President was assassinated by a precision guerrilla team of at least seven men, including anti-Castro adventurers and members

of the paramilitary right. Of course, the Ministry of Truth concluded—by scrupulously ignoring the most compelling evidence and carefully selecting only those facts that conformed to its preconceived thesis of a lone assassin—that "no credible evidence suggests that the shots were fired from . . . any place other than the Texas School Book Depository Building." But anyone who takes the time to read the Warren Report will find that of the witnesses in Dealey Plaza who were able to assess the origin of the shots, almost two thirds said they came from the grassy-knoll area in front and to the right of the Presidential limousine and not from the Book Depository, which was to the rear of the President. A number of reliable witnesses testified that they heard shots ring out from behind the picket fence and saw a puff of smoke drift into the air. Additional evidence supporting this can be found in the [Abraham] Zapruder film published in *Life*, which reveals that the President was slammed backward by the impact of a bullet; unless you abrogate Newton's third law of motion, this means the President was shot from the front. Also—though they were contradicted later—several of the doctors at Parkland Hospital who examined the President's neck wound contended it was an entrance wound, which would certainly tend to indicate that Kennedy was shot from the front. In the course of our investigation, we've uncovered additional evidence establishing absolutely that there were at least four men on the grassy knoll, at least two behind the picket fence and two or more behind a small stone wall to the right of the fence. As I reconstruct it from the still-incomplete evidence in our possession, one man fired at the President from each location, while the role of his companion was to snatch up the cartridges as they were ejected. . . .

---

*He had nitrates on both hands, but no nitrates on his cheek.*

---

It seems virtually certain that the cartridges, along with the rifles, were then thrown into the trunk of a car—parked directly behind the picket fence—which was driven from the scene some hours after the assassination. If there had been a thorough search of all vehicles in the vicinity of the grassy knoll immediately after the assassination, this incriminating evidence might have been uncovered—along with the real authors of the President's murder. In addition to the assassins on the grassy knoll, at least two other men fired from behind the President, one from the Book Depository Building—not Oswald—and one, in all probability, from the Dal-Tex Building. As it happens, a man was arrested right after the assassination as he left the Dal-Tex Building and was taken away in a patrol car, but like the three other men detained after the assassination—one in the railroad yard behind the grassy knoll, one on the railroad overpass farther down the parade route, and one in front of the Book Depository Building—he then dropped out of sight completely. All of these suspects taken into custody after the assassination remain as anonymous as if they'd been detained for throwing a candy wrapper on the sidewalk. We have also located another man—in green combat fatigues—who was not involved in the shooting but created a diversionary action in order to distract people's attention from the snipers. This individual screamed, fell to the ground and simulated an epileptic fit, drawing people away from the vicinity of the knoll just before the President's motorcade reached the ambush point. So you have at least seven people involved, with four firing at the President and catching him in a crossfire. . . .

---

*This weapon was taken from the building approximately 20 minutes before Oswald's.*

---

It was a precision operation and was carried out coolly and with excellent coordination; the assassins even kept in contact by radio. The President, of course, had no chance. It was an overkill operation. As far as the actual sequence of shots goes, you'll remember that the Warren Commission concluded that only three bullets were fired at the President—one that hit just below the back of his neck, exited through his throat and then passed through Governor Connally's body; one that missed; and one that blew off a portion of the President's skull and killed him. Like most of the other conclusions of the Commission, this one contradicts both the evidence and the testimony of eyewitnesses. The initial shot hit the President in the front of the neck, as the Parkland Hospital doctors recognized—though they were later contradicted by the military physicians at the Bethesda autopsy, and by the Warren Report. The second shot struck the President in the back; the location of this wound can be verified not by consulting the official autopsy report—on which the Commission based its conclusion that this bullet hit Kennedy in the back of the neck and exited from his throat—but by perusing the reports filed by two FBI agents who were present at the President's autopsy in Bethesda, Maryland. Both stated unequivocally that the bullet in question entered President Kennedy's back and did not continue through his body. I also refer you to a photograph of the President's shirt taken by the FBI, and to a drawing of the President's back wound made by one of the examining physicians at Bethesda; the location of the wound in both cases corresponds exactly—more than three inches below the President's neck. Yet the Commission concluded that this wound occurred in his neck. This, of course, was to make it more believable that the same bullet had exited from the President's throat and slanted on down through Governor Connally. Even if this bullet had entered where the Commission claims and then exited from the President's throat, it would have been possible for it to enter Governor Connally's upper back at a downward angle, exit from his lower chest and lodge finally in his thigh—fired, as the Commission says it was, from the elevation of the sixth-floor window of the Book Depository—only if Connally had been sitting in the President's lap or if the bullet had de-scribed two 90-degree turns on its way from President Kennedy's throat to Governor Connally's back. Clearly, the President's throat wound was caused by the first shot, this one from the grassy knoll in front of the limousine; and his back wound came from the rear. I've already given you my reasons for reaching this conclusion.

## Bullet Fragments and Exhibit 399

*Playboy: If the first bullet was fired from the front, why wasn't it found in the President's body, or somewhere in the Presidential limousine?*

*Garrison:* The exact nature of the President's wounds, as well as the disposition of the bullets or bullet fragments, are among the many concealed items in this case. I told you ear-lier about the men on the grassy knoll whose sole function we believe was to catch the cartridges as they were ejected from the assassins' rifles. We also have reason to suspect that other members of the conspiracy may have been assigned the job of removing other evidence—such as traceable bullet fragments—that might betray the assassins. In the chaos of November 22nd, this would not have been as difficult as it sounds. We know that a bullet, designated Exhibit number 399 by the Warren Commission, was planted on a stretcher in Parkland Hospital to incriminate Oswald. The Commission concluded that this bullet allegedly hit both Kennedy and Governor Connally, causing seven wounds and breaking three bones—and emerged without a dent! In subsequent ballistics tests with the same gun, every bullet was squashed completely out of shape from impact with various simulated human targets. So, if the conspirators could fabricate a bullet, they could easily conceal one. But to return to the sequence of shots: Governor Connally was struck by a third bullet—as he himself insisted, not the one that struck Kennedy in the back—also fired from the rear. A fourth shot missed the Presidential limousine completely and struck the curb along the south side of Main Street, disintegrating into fragments; the trajectory of this bullet has been plotted backward to a point of origin in the Dal-Tex Building. The fifth shot, which struck the President in the right temple, tore off the top of his skull and snapped him back into his seat—a point overlooked by the Warren Commission—had to have been fired from the grassy knoll. There is also medical evidence indicating the likelihood that an additional head shot may have been fired. The report of Dr. Robert McClelland at Parkland Hospital, for example, states that "the cause of death was due to massive head and brain injury from a gunshot wound of the left temple." And yet another shot may also have been fired; frames 208 to 211 of the Zapruder film, which were deleted from the Warren Report—presumably as irrelevant—reveal signs of stress appearing suddenly on the back of a street sign momentarily obstructing the view between the grassy knoll and the President's car. These stress signs may very well have been caused by the impact of a stray bullet on the sign. We'll never be sure about this, however, because the day after the assassination, the sign was removed and no one in Dallas seems to know what became of it. Some of the gunmen appear to have used frangible bullets, a variant of the dumdum bullet that is forbidden by the Geneva Treaty.

Frangible bullets explode on impact into tiny fragments, as did the bullet that caused the fatal wound in the President's head. Of course, frangible bullets are ideal in a political assassination, because they almost guarantee massive damage and assure that no tangible evidence will remain that ballistics experts could use to trace the murder weapon. I might also mention that frangible bullets cannot be fired from a Mannlicher-Carcano, such as the Commission concludes Oswald used to kill the President. Also parenthetically, this type of bullet was issued by the CIA for use in anti-Castro-exile raids on Cuba. In summation, there were at least five or six shots fired at the President from front and rear by at least four gunmen, assisted by several accomplices, two of whom probably picked up the cartridges and one of whom created a diversion to draw people's eyes away from the grassy knoll. At this stage of events, Lee Harvey Oswald was no more than a spectator to the assassination—perhaps in a very literal sense. As the first shot rang out, Associated Press photographer James Altgens snapped a picture of the motorcade that shows a man with a remarkable resemblance to Lee Harvey Oswald—same hairline, same face shape—standing in the doorway of the Book Depository Building. Somehow or other, the Warren Commission concluded that this man was actually Billy Nolan Lovelady, an employee of the Depository, who looked very little like Oswald. Furthermore, on the day of the assassination, Oswald was wearing a white T-shirt under a long-sleeved dark shirt opened halfway to his waist—the same outfit worn by the man in the doorway—but Lovelady said that on November 22nd he was wearing a short-sleeved, red-and-white-striped sport shirt buttoned near the neck. The Altgens photograph indicates the very real possibility that at the moment Oswald was supposed to have been crouching in the sixth-floor window of the Depository shooting Kennedy, he may actually have been standing outside the front door watching the Presidential motorcade.

# 4

# Kennedy's Policy on Vietnam Led to His Murder

L. Fletcher Prouty

Colonel L. Fletcher Prouty, a retired Air Force officer who served in the Pentagon, explores government documents and events that point to a U.S. government plot to assassinate President John F. Kennedy. Prouty contends that government officials had Kennedy killed in order to stop him from implementing his plan to disengage from Vietnam. Just four days before Kennedy's death, his cabinet was flown to Hawaii to discuss topics that were not currently a part of Kennedy's Vietnam policy, but became part of Lyndon B. Johnson's policy once he replaced Kennedy. Prouty cites this meeting and other facts as circumstantial evidence that proves the existence of a conspiracy to kill Kennedy.

It is my belief that the policy announced so forcefully by [President John F.] Kennedy in his earlier NSAM [National [Security Action Memorandum] #55 and in NSAM #263 had been the major factor in causing the decision by certain elements of the power elite to do away with Kennedy before his reelection and to take control of the U.S. government in the process.

Kennedy's NSAM #263 policy would have assured that Americans by the hundreds of thousands would not have been sent to the war in Vietnam. This policy was anathema

L. Fletcher Prouty, *JFK: The CIA, Vietnam, and the Plot to Assassinate John F. Kennedy*. New York: Carol Publishing Group, 1992. Copyright © 1992 by L. Fletcher Prouty. Reproduced by permission.

to elements of the military-industrial complex, their bankers, and their allies in the government. This policy and the almost certain fact that Kennedy would be reelected President in 1964 set the stage for the plot to assassinate him. . . .

---

*This policy was anathema to elements of the military-industrial complex.*

---

First of all, NSAM #263, October 11, 1963, was a crucial White House document. Much of it, guided by White House policy, was actually written by my boss in the Pentagon, General [Victor] Krulak, myself, and others of his staff. I am familiar with it and with events which led to its creation. . . .

## The Missing Enclosure

In order to appreciate what had taken place with the publication of President Kennedy's policy I shall cite the few paragraphs of this NSAM #263 (Document 146 in the *Pentagon Papers*)

> At a meeting on October 5, 1963, the President considered the recommendations contained in the report of Secretary [of Defense Robert S.] McNamara and General [Maxwell] Taylor [chairman of the Joint Chiefs of Staff] on their mission to South Vietnam.
>
> The President approved the military recommendations contained in Section I B (1-3) of the report, but directed that no formal announcement be made of the implementation of plans to withdraw 1,000 U.S. military personnel by the end of 1963.
>
> After discussion of the remaining recommendations of the report, the President approved an instruction to Ambassador [Henry Cabot] Lodge which is set forth in State Department telegram No. 534 to Saigon.

What is unusual about this cover letter from McGeorge Bundy [John F. Kennedy's special assistant for national security affairs] is the fact that, although it makes reference to the McNamara-Taylor report, it does not carry or cite an enclosure. Without the report itself in the record this cover letter of NSAM #263 is all but worthless. This fact has confused researchers since that time. The cover letter authenticates the fact that the President had approved only "Section I B (1-3) of the report." In other words, on that date, that was an official statement of the President's Vietnam policy. What does that section say? In the usual source documents of the Pentagon Papers the researcher will have to turn to another section to find Document 142, "Report of McNamara-Taylor Mission to South Vietnam." Here he will discover the cited sections (pertinent items extracted below):

> IB(2) A program be established to train Vietnamese so that essential functions now performed by U.S. military personnel can be carried out by Vietnamese by the end of 1965. It should be possible to withdraw the bulk of U.S. military personnel by that time.

> IB(3) In accordance with the program to train progressively Vietnamese to take over military functions, the Defense Department should announce in the very near future presently prepared plans to withdraw 1,000 U.S. military personnel by the end of 1963.

In brief, those sections above are the essence of the Kennedy policy that would take men out of Vietnam in 1963 and the bulk of all military personnel out by 1965. At that time, after nearly a generation of involvement in Vietnam, this was a clear signal that Kennedy meant to disengage American military men from Vietnam. This was the bomb-shell. It made headlines around the world. . . .

---

*"The Defense Department should announce . . . presently prepared plans to withdraw 1,000 U.S. military personnel by the end of 1963."*

---

Our history books and the basic sources of history which lie buried in the archives of government documents have been concealed from the public and, worse still, government documents have been tampered with and forged. As I have just demonstrated above, this most important policy statement, NSAM #263, that so many historians and journalists say does not exist, has been divided into two sections in the Pentagon Papers source history. One section is no more than the simple cover letter, and the other section, pages away in the record, is presented by its simple title as a "report" with no cross-reference whatsoever to the fact that it is the basic substance of President Kennedy's Vietnam policy. Such things are no accident. The record of the Kennedy administration has been savagely distorted in basic government documents and by so-called historians who have accepted the myths to be found on the record.

---

*The record of the Kennedy administration has been savagely distorted.*

---

I have cited these facts with care in order to demonstrate what the original presidential policy was and to compare it with what has been done with it since those days by those who wish to conceal and obfuscate the facts of the Kennedy administration by means of such grandiose "cover story" creations as the *Pentagon Papers*, the *Report of the Warren Commission*, and the whole family of historical publications both from governmental and private sources. As we have seen repeatedly, the cover-story aspect of the plot to kill the President is much the more serious and elaborate task of the whole plan. . . .

## Distortions of History

When the "Department of Defense Study of American Decisionmaking on Vietnam," as the *Pentagon Papers* study is called officially, was completed in January 1969, it was said to be highly classified and did not become available to the public until Daniel Ellsberg, who had worked in Vietnam . . . , found a way to make the documents available to certain major newspapers in June 1971. While the Nixon administration was bringing charges against Ellsberg and the newspapers in order to suppress their use, Senator Mike Gravel obtained a complete set of these documents and, over a period of days, read them into the *Congressional Record* as a way of making them available to the public.

In his introduction to this four-volume compilation Senator Gravel said:

> The Pentagon Papers tell of the purposeful withholding and distortion of facts. There are no military secrets to be found here, only an appalling litany of faulty premises and questionable objectives, built one

upon the other over the course of four administrations, and perpetuated today by a fifth administration.

The Pentagon Papers show that we have created, in the last quarter century, a new culture, a national security culture, protected from the influences of American life by the shield of secrecy.

This was 1971. In 1991, after time enough to permit government historians to correct the brazen errors and omissions of the record of the Vietnam era, the Office of the Historian in the Bureau of Public Affairs of the Department of State has published a new document, "Vietnam August–December 1963." Even in this new publication, the presentation of NSAM #263 is unclear. On page 395 it publishes document #194, National Security Action Memorandum #263 in the form presented above. Then without any cross-referencing data whatsoever, on page 336, it presents Document #167: Memorandum From the Chairman of the Joint Chiefs of Staff (Taylor) and the Secretary of Defense (McNamara) to the President, Subject: Report of McNamara–Taylor Mission to South Vietnam. Then to further obfuscate the record, this State Department publication omits crucial elements of the trip report entirely. Instead of improving the historical record with the passage of time, the authors are further distorting it. There can be but one conclusion. Almost three decades later the cover story lives on, and records of the Kennedy era, in particular, are the hardest hit. . . .

## McNamara's Task Force

In an ominous way, the Pentagon Papers and Watergate episodes were cut from the same fabric, and most important, their exposure was a direct outgrowth of the nationwide dissatisfaction with the Vietnam War. Because the development of the war in Indochina had been spread out so long, since 1945, and because most of the events that brought about this terrible form of modern genocide in the name of "anticommunism" or "containment" were buried in deep secrecy or not even available in written records, Robert S. McNamara, then secretary of defense, directed, on June 17, 1967, that a task force be formed to collate and study the history of U.S. involvement in Vietnam from World War II to the present. . . .

I have used various editions of the Pentagon Papers as

reference material. They are useful and they are quite accurate as far as individual documents go, but they are dangerous in the hands of those who do not have the experience or the other sources required to validate and balance their content. This is because their true source was only marginally the Pentagon and because the clever selection of those documents by the compilers removed many important papers. This neglect of key documents served to reduce the value of those that remained to tell the story of the Vietnam War. From the beginning, the Pentagon Papers were a compilation of documents designed to paint President John F. Kennedy as the villain of the story, and to shield the role of the CIA.

This vast stack of papers has been labeled the Pentagon Papers, but that is a misnomer. It is quite true that most of them were found in certain highly classified files in the Pentagon, but they were functionally limited files. For example, despite their volume—nearly four thousand documents—there are remarkably few that actually bear the signature of military officers. In fact, many of those that carry the signature of a military officer, or that refer to military officers, make reference to such men as Edward G. Lansdale, who actually worked for the CIA while serving in a cover assignment with the military. When such papers are removed from the "military" or "Pentagon" categorization, what remains is a nonmilitary and non-Pentagon collection. For the serious and honest historian, this becomes an important distinction. To be truly "Pentagon" Papers, the majority of them, at least, ought to have been written there. . . .

---

*"There are . . . only an appalling litany of faulty premises and questionable objectives."*

---

This reveals one of my greatest misgivings concerning the accuracy of the study. There are altogether too many important papers that did not get included in this study, too many that were absolutely crucial to an understanding of the origins of, and reasons for, this war.

This has been a complaint of historians who have attempted to teach the facts of this war. They have found that the history book accounts of it have been written by writers who were not there, who had little or nothing to do with it—or, conversely, that they have been written by those who were there, but who were there for a one-year tour of duty, usually in the post-1965 period. Few of these writers have had the comprehensive experience that is a prerequisite to understanding that type of contemporary history.

---

*The Pentagon Papers and Watergate episodes were cut from the same fabric.*

---

Regarding the Pentagon Papers themselves, Senator Gravel wrote:

> The Papers do not support our good intentions. The Papers prove that, from the beginning, the war has been an American war, serving to perpetuate American military power in Asia. Peace has never been on the American agenda for Southeast Asia. Neither we nor the South Vietnamese have been masters of our Southeast Asian policy; we have been its victims, as the leaders of America sought to preserve their reputation for toughness and determination. . . .

## Change in Vietnam Policy

It is important to understand the Pentagon Papers' subtle anti-Kennedy slant. Nothing reveals this bias more than the following extract taken from the section "The Overthrow of Ngo Dinh Diem, May–November 1963."

At the end of a crucial summary of the most momentous ninety-day period in modern American history, from August 22 to November 22, 1963, this is what the authors of the Pentagon Papers had to say:

> After having delayed an appropriate period, the U.S. recognized the new government on November 8. As the euphoria wore off, however, the real gravity of the economic situation and the lack of expertise in the new government became apparent to both Vietnamese and American officials. The deterioration of the military situation and the Strategic Hamlet program also came more and more clearly into perspective.

> These topics dominated the discussions at the Honolulu conference on November 20 when [Henry

Cabot] Lodge and the country team [from Vietnam] met with [Dean] Rusk, [Robert] McNamara, [Maxwell] Taylor, [George] Ball, and [McGeorge] Bundy. But the meeting ended inconclusively. After Lodge had conferred with the President a few days later in Washington, the White House tried to pull together some conclusions and offer some guidance for our continuing and now deeper involvement in Vietnam. The instructions contained in NSAM 273, however, did not reflect the truly dire situation as it was to come to light in succeeding weeks. The reappraisals forced by the new information would swiftly make it irrelevant as it was overtaken by events.

Recall what had been going on during that month of November 1963. President Ngo Dinh Diem and his brother had been murdered, and the administration of South Vietnam had been placed in the hands of Gen. Duong Van "Big" Minh. Then, in one of the strangest scenarios of recent history, most of the members of the Kennedy cabinet had flown to Honolulu, together, for that November 20 series of conferences. The full cabinet meeting—even the secretary of agriculture was there—in Hawaii was to be followed by a flight to Tokyo on November 22. Again, almost all of the Kennedy cabinet members were on that flight to Tokyo. They were on that aircraft bound for Tokyo when they learned that President Kennedy had been shot dead in Dallas. Upon receipt of that stunning news, they ordered the plane to return directly to Hawaii and, almost immediately, on to Washington.

But consider here the strange and impersonal words used by this "official history." The Pentagon Papers, in its long section on the events of that tragic period, ends its own narrative report of those events by saying: "But probably more important, the deterioration of the military situation of the Vietnamese position. . . ."

News of this "White House Report" was splashed across the front page of the U.S. armed forces *Pacific Stars and Stripes* newspaper of October 4, 1963, in banner headlines: U.S. TROOPS SEEN OUT OF VIET BY '65.

These are quotes taken from official documents of that time, all taking an optimistic view of the war by the leaders closest to it and including statements by President Kennedy and President Diem. The official Kennedy White House policy document, National Security Action Memorandum #263, was dated October 11, 1963, and there is no evidence that the situation, as perceived by Kennedy and his closest advisers, had changed over the next month. General Krulak was as close to the President and his policy as he had ever been, and I worked directly with General Krulak on the Joint Staff. We never heard of any changes in plans from the White House.

---

*"Peace has never been on the American agenda for Southeast Asia."*

---

Just four days after Kennedy's death and less than sixty days after Kennedy published NSAM #263, which visualized the Vietnamization of the war and the return of all American personnel by the end of 1965, Lyndon Johnson and most of the JFK cabinet viewed the situation in an entirely different light. In Johnson's NSAM #273 they saw the military situation deteriorating ("the deterioration of . . . the Strategic Hamlet program") and all of a sudden saw the program as a failure. ("These topics dominated the discussions at the Honolulu Conference on November 20. . . .")

## The Plot Thickens

This is a remarkable statement. On that date, John Kennedy was still alive and President of the United States. Yet this report says that his cabinet had been assembled in Honolulu to discuss "these topics"—the very same topics of NSAM #273, dated November 26, and a vital step on the way to a total reversal of Kennedy's own policy, as stated in the Taylor-McNamara report and in NSAM #263, dated October 2, 1963. The total reversal was completed with the publication of NSAM #288, March 26, 1964.

This situation cannot be treated lightly. How did it happen that the Kennedy cabinet had traveled to Hawaii at precisely the same time Kennedy was touring in Texas? How did it happen that the subject of discussion in Hawaii, before JFK was killed, was a strange agenda that would not come up in the White House until after he had been murdered? Who could have known, beforehand, that this new—non-Kennedy—agenda would be needed in the White House because Kennedy would no longer be President?

Is there any possibility that the "powers that be" who planned and executed the Kennedy assassination had also been able to get the Kennedy cabinet out of the country and to have them conferring in Hawaii on an agenda that would be put before President Lyndon Johnson just four days after Kennedy's death?

President Kennedy would not have sent his cabinet to Hawaii to discuss that agenda. He had issued his own agenda for Vietnam on October 11, 1963, and he had no reason to change it. More than that, he had no reason at all to send them all to Hawaii for such a conference. It is never good practice for a President to have key members of his cabinet out of town while he is on an extended trip. Why was the cabinet in Hawaii? Who ordered the cabinet members there? If JFK had no reason to send them to Hawaii, who did, and why?

---

*We never heard of any changes in plans from the White House.*

---

Keep in mind, through this series of vitally important questions, that we are piling circumstance upon circumstance. It is the body of circumstantial evidence that proves the existence of conspiracy. . . .

These questions and the subjects they unfold are the things of which assassinations and coups d'état are made. The plotters worked out their plans in detail as they moved to take over the government that Kennedy had taken from them. As a result, every other public official became a pawn on that master chess board. Assassinations and coups d'état permeate and threaten all levels of society. . . .

It seems that those who planned the murder of the President knew the inner workings of the government very well. This fact is made evident not so much by the skill with which the murder of the President was undertaken as by the masterful cover-up program that has continued since November 22, 1963, and that terrible hour in Dallas's Dealey Plaza when the warfare in Indochina moved from a low-intensity conflict, as seen by President Kennedy, to a major operation—a major war—in the hands of the Johnson administration.

# 5

# The Armchair Theorists Lack Credibility

Richard Warren Lewis

Writing five years after John F. Kennedy's death, Richard Warren Lewis explores the findings and claims made by JFK assassination buffs. Lewis questions the credibility of their claims
and debunks rumors that these "scavengers" have dug up. He
frowns upon these amateur detectives, claiming they are out to
undermine the Warren Commission's case. In particular, Lewis
addresses the work of Vincent Salandria. After reviewing by-
stander Abraham Zapruder's motion-picture film of the event,
Salandria produced evidence against the lone-assassin theory of
the commission. Lewis proceeds to disprove Salandria's theory
with his own research. David Lifton, a graduate student of
UCLA, enlarged sections of photographs taken on the day of
the assassination and located several forms he interpreted as assassins firing at the motorcade. Lewis points out Lifton's limitations in understanding photography, discrediting his findings.
Lewis believes these "superbuffs" see what they want to see; he
presents these assassination researchers as frenzied controversy-
mongers who will not stop until they find a second assassin.

---

The numbing wreckage wrought by the fourth Presidential assassination within a century has washed up a curious assortment of flotsam and jetsam. Chain letters from
assassination buffs circulate around the country, seeking au-
tographs of all the witnesses to the killing. Automobiles flout
bumper stickers reading "Lee Harvey Oswald—Where Are

Richard Warren Lewis, *The Endless Paradox: The Scavengers and Critics of the Warren Report*. New York: Delacorte Press, 1967. Copyright © 1967 by Alskog Inc.
and Richard Warren Lewis. Reproduced by permission of Dell Publishing, a division of Random House, Inc.

You Now That We Need You?" and "Who Murdered Kennedy?"

But the strongest wave has deposited a foamy ground swell of amateur detectives who passionately believe that one deranged individual could not have possibly murdered someone of such stature as the late President. Only a conspiracy, they say, could have arranged an act so senseless. The doubters keep vigil at the National Archives in Washington, D.C., hoping for new shards of information to bolster their special interests. They re-enact ballistics tests and run down even the most inconsequential evidence in an effort to undermine the Commission's case. They pass photographs, maps and documents among themselves on a throbbing party line of speculation and rumor. "Mark Lane's making a lot of noise now," says one of the superbuffs, "but he's not in on the new string that's developing."

---

*They re-enact ballistics tests and run down even the most inconsequential evidence in an effort to undermine the Commission's case.*

---

These latest conspiracy advocates have become heirs apparent to the early critics such as Richard Popkin, a philosophy professor at the San Diego branch of the University of California. Popkin contended that there were actually two assassins, the alleged killer plus someone who impersonated him and left a trail of incriminating evidence. His book, *The Second Oswald*, reads like potential source material for Alfred Hitchcock. Thomas Buchanan, an ex-Communist American expatriate currently employed as a computer technician in Paris, earlier had suggested that the assassination had been masterminded by Mr. X—a right-wing Texas oil baron who feared Kennedy's oil-depletion-allowance policies. His book, *Who Killed Kennedy?*, gained wide acceptance in the European mind during 1965.

The successors to Buchanan and Popkin (as well as Lane, [*Inquest* author Edward J.] Epstein *et al.*) have aired their doubts mostly in articles published by limited-circulation magazines. But their theories have gained far greater currency than they might have years before merely because of the existing climate of doubt and confusion caused by their predecessors.

## The Zapruder Film

One of the more strident *nouvelle vague* voices belongs to Vincent Salandria, a crewcut Philadelphia lawyer and consultant to the American Civil Liberties Union. On a four-day visit to the National Archives, Salandria conducted an exhaustive study of the [Abraham] Zapruder motion-picture film. He placed two slide projectors side by side, superimposed pictures of the President suffering his mortal head wound, and discovered that the President's head moved backward and to the left. The Commission had stated that the bullet ". . . entered the right-rear portion of his head, causing a massive and fatal wound."

Salandria has hammered home this apparent head-snap discrepancy in speaking engagements and magazine articles ever since. Since he never accepts any form of payment for public appearances, his motives would seem to be altruistic.

"Once the American people is [sic] permitted to see what it has a right and duty to see in a society which is still open, to wit: the Zapruder photographic documentation of the rude manner in which their President was dispatched from this world by a team of assassins," says Salandria, "then the lone assassin theory of the Warren Commission will be reduced to the proper place it deserves in history as patent pap—improper sustenance for free minds. The Zapruder films show interalia that the President was propelled, pounded and pivoted—his whole body was—as a limp, dead thing, smashed abruptly backward and leftward by the force of a bullet aimed from the front and right of him, to wit from the grassy knoll area.

---

*Salandria ignores the most important evidence.*

---

"The speed of the movement and the direction backward cannot be explained as a result of voluntary or involuntary self-propulsion, or any force impinging from the rear. The frames which follow 313 demonstrate that this thumping of the President leftward and backward results in a continuous progression which pounds him to the back of the limousine seat and then bounces him off the seat into his wife's lap. What did the Warren Commission see fit to say about this, the most dramatic phenomenon of the assassination? Not a single word was directed to this problem. This silence speaks most eloquently for the Commission's true function. When these films are released, the process of keeping lie upon lie to shore up the punctured single assassin theory will end."

## Evidence to the Contrary

Salandria ignores the most important evidence, which is the initial direction and first movement of the President's head when the fatal bullet struck. "The initial motion of his head is downward in frames 312–313," states Dr. R.A.J. Riddle, Assistant Professor of Physics at UCLA and a member of the university's Brain Research Institute. Dr. Riddle commented further when asked if the head movement was consistent with a shot fired from the grassy-knoll area. "The initial motion of the head is consistent with a bullet fired from an elevation of about twenty-five degrees or more."

But further investigation shows that the extreme top of the knoll is approximately eleven degrees from a horizontal plane at the approximate height of the President's head. There is no possible firing position at "twenty-five degrees or more" in that area. There exists only open sky.

The initial downward movement is consistent with a shot fired from fifteen degrees *behind* the President's head. The sixth-floor window of the Texas School Book Depository lies at fifteen degrees elevation.

---

*The instantaneous reaction to that bullet was impossible to record on Zapruder's camera.*

---

Where Salandria emphasizes the "thumping" which occurs in Zapruder frames 314–320, it is not central to what has already transpired in frames 312–313. In frame 312 the President's head has already slumped over from the effects of the bullet that went through his neck. He is practically resting in his wife's arms. According to Mrs. Kennedy's testimony, she had already begun to pull his body toward her at this juncture. She is cradling him. His head hangs downward. The point of his chin is nearly resting on his chest, probably near the nadir of its downward arc.

The President's head had not been hit by frame 312. The impact from the fatal bullet striking the right rear of his skull (as the sniper would have seen it) definitely occurs between frames 312 and 313, a period of about 1/36th of a second. In frame 313, he has been hit and his head is clearly forced downward as far as possible. . . .

With a bullet traveling so fast, the instantaneous reaction to that bullet was impossible to record on Zapruder's camera. Consequently no one knows the precise instant the bullet struck the President. Only the effect of the bullet can be seen. There is no doubt, however, that the President's head moved forward and down from its original position in 312. . . .

## Proof of Snipers?

Harold Feldman, a bespectacled high-school teacher of foreign languages, works closely with Salandria, who is his brother-in-law. Footnotes in his own articles cite Salandria's previous work. They have visited Dallas together, huffed and puffed across Oswald's escape route, and talked at length with Mrs. Marguerite Oswald, the mother of the assassin. . . .

One of Feldman's prime contributions to the cause of the superbuffs was his Dealey Plaza inventory.

"I analyzed the testimony of 129 witnesses to the assassination to find out where they felt the shots were coming from," says Feldman. "I tell how the Warren Commission makes them appear as though they were telling an opposite story from the one they're actually telling. The very witnesses thought these bullets came from the grassy knoll. The Warren Commission actually disagrees with the majority of witnesses and we agree with them." The "we's" include Mark Lane, who has adopted Feldman's survey for his own.

Lane, however, has steered clear of a related survey undertaken by David Lifton, a twenty-five-year-old graduate student in engineering at UCLA. His census of the trees visible on the grassy knoll on the day of the assassination conflicts with the number of trees existing today. According to Lifton, one tree is missing. He theorizes that an artificial tree was installed on Dealey Plaza, prior to the assassination, and that camouflaged snipers who might have hit Kennedy were concealed beneath it.

To further document this amazing find, he enlarged, up to twenty times their original size, sections of photographs taken from the twenty-six volumes [of the Warren Commission Report] and various periodicals. The photographs have been blown up completely beyond reality. In the shrubbery of the grassy knoll he has located several forms which he interprets as assassins firing at the motorcade. One of them looks as if he is wearing a Kaiser Wilhelm helmet. Others wear electronic headsets and man periscopes and machine guns on a platform operated by hydraulic lifts. One of his imagined finds resembles General Douglas MacArthur. None of these illusions is visible on the original prints.

The visions are caused by Lifton's limitations in understanding basic photographic techniques. When he enlarges these photographs from the printed page, or from copies of the original prints, in most cases he is actually enlarging engraving dots rather than the original photographic grain and tone. Critical detail, for even the most simple analysis, is lost in this naïve method of enlargement, so that everything appears out of context—an eye-boggling maze of literally thousands of reproduction dots.

Though these recent theories of Lifton's may be quickly discredited, he did achieve widespread kudos among the critics by establishing that two frames of Zapruder film printed in the twenty-six volumes were reversed, thereby confusing the sequence of events following Kennedy's mortal skull wound. Lifton and other critics like Raymond Marcus had jumped to the conclusion that this was done intentionally to alter the movements of the President's head after the crucial Zapruder frame 313. A printing error actually transposed the two engravings. A friend of Lifton's received a letter of acknowledgment from FBI Chief J. Edgar Hoover, explaining that his find was authentic. [Lifton actually wrote the letter to Hoover using his friend's name.]

Since that moment of glory Lifton has become consumed with invalidating other evidence offered by the Commission. To demonstrate that the pristine bullet found on Governor Connally's stretcher was incapable of inflicting the indicated damage to both Kennedy and Connally, he purchased a Mannlicher-Carcano rifle and some 6.5-millimeter metal-jacketed military cartridges of the type manufactured by the Western Cartridge Company. He also obtained a twelve-foot-thick piece of foam rubber, which he hoped would halt his fusillade of bullets and then allow him to observe their spent condition. Lifton drove to a secluded area near the Pacific Ocean and fired away. The bullets, unfortunately, rebounded from the rubber backstop. The large majority of them were never found.

## The Telling Sign

Undaunted, Lifton has distributed scale-drawn maps of Dealey Plaza among fellow superbuffs, along with charts indicating where various witnesses to the assassination were located. At the same time he has advanced another one of his fanciful speculations. In analyzing the Zapruder motion-picture film, Lifton has determined that stress marks are visible on an Elm Street roadside sign reading "NO TURNS." The sign is located directly between Zapruder's camera position and a critical moment of the Presidential motorcade. Lifton feels that these marks were caused by an errant bullet striking the sign from a position in front of the motorcade, thereby indicating the existence of an additional assassin.

"*I* want to be a famous author like all those other people," says Lifton, who since has co-authored a magazine article entitled "The Case for Three Assassins." With his wild speculations, he just might get his wish.

"Dave Lifton's theory [about the stress marks on the sign] happens to be a theory that I disagree with," says Raymond Marcus, a Los Angeles distributor of signs reading "FOR SALE," "BEWARE OF DOG" and "FOR RENT." "I've seen evidence that leads me to believe that it's not correct. I have seen the films at the Archives. I've studied them very carefully and I am convinced that those are not stress lines on the sign, but stress lines on the film itself which a photo expert told me, in his opinion, was caused by the fact that there's a splice [in the film] just preceding them. Double thickness of film going through the sprocket of the projector caused the stress lines. There was a cluster of people standing immediately in front of the sign. It would be highly probable that one of them would have been hit, and, if not hit, they certainly would have heard the noise of a bullet whacking into the sign. This does not in any way rule out the possibility that the sign was hit. I don't want you to knock it off just because I'm against it."

## The Authenticity of Bullet 399

Marcus is the author of *The Bastard Bullet*, a lengthy monograph printed in photographic offset and described in a preface by Penn Jones as "an outstanding piece of research . . . should be required reading for all college logic students, and all others interested in the assassination of President Kennedy." . . .

Marcus is a self-styled specialist on Bullet 399, the projectile which wounded both the President and Governor Connally.

Almost every theorist questions the undistorted appearance of Exhibit (bullet) 399. Its head seems to be unflattened—an apparent contradiction to the damage it accomplished.

"Bullet 399 is not a legitimate assassination bullet at all," Marcus declares. "It was never fired at any human target. Instead, it was deliberately fired in such a manner as to prevent its mutilation. And then, with the intention of assuring its identification with the Mannlicher-Carcano rifle allegedly belonging to Lee Harvey Oswald, it was planted by person or persons unknown on the hospital stretcher where it was subsequently 'found.'"

---

*Lifton has become consumed with invalidating other evidence offered by the Commission.*

---

Expert analyses by agencies independent of the Commission have determined that the approximate grains of metal lost by Exhibit 399 are entirely consistent with the particle of the projectile remaining in Connally's body. "The tests performed indicate that after it would go through a substance similar to the President's neck it would be in perfect condition with perhaps a light amount of wobble, but only a very slight amount," says Arlen Specter, the Commission counsel who worked in this area. "The tests performed on anesthetized goats suggest that a bullet would be flattened on grazing a rib such as was grazed in Governor Connally's body in a fashion that 399 would sustain. The amount of metallic deposit in the Governor's wrist and a small piece of metal in the thigh are completely consistent with the metallic substance which was lost by the bullet identified as Exhibit 399. The most precise estimates which could be given were those advanced by Dr. Gregory, who is the orthopedic surgeon who operated on Governor Connally's wrist, and he testified that the deposits in the wrist would have to be weighed in micrograms, which is the equivalent of a postage stamp. So that while unusual, it is entirely consistent with all the known facts that the bullet identified as Exhibit 399 did pass through the President's neck, did graze the Governor's rib, did tumble through his rib and ultimately lodged in a superficial flesh wound in his left thigh."

## The Planted Bullet

If somebody was going to plant a bullet to frame Oswald, he would have been foolish to plant a near pristine bullet—which could only increase suspicion. There was no way of knowing in advance whether the President would be killed on Elm Street, taken to Parkland Hospital or rushed to Air Force One waiting at Love Field. The only individuals who could have planted such a bullet would have been members of the President's personal staff or Secret Service agents attending the President, all highly unlikely subjects to a conspiracy.

Those who cling to the fact that the bullet was planted on a stretcher in Parkland Hospital as part of a conspiracy fail to note that the bullet matches ballistically to the fragments found in the President's limousine. If the bullet was indeed planted, then the fragments would had to have been planted as well. And if one believes that both the bullet and its fragments were planted, it is impossible to explain what happened to the bullets that struck both Kennedy and Connally.

## A Photographic Fraud

Like other superbuffs, the thirty-nine-year-old Marcus has become fascinated with the art of photography. He has isolated rectangular inch-square segments from the Zapruder frames printed in *Life* magazine and enlarged them to eight times their original size. He then distributed these blowups among fellow skeptics to prove that the first bullet struck the President substantially before the moment indicated by the Warren Commission, thereby implying the existence of a second assassin—in the Dallas County Courts Building one block south of Dealey Plaza. An analysis of other photographs of the President's limousine taken at the moment Marcus claims the President was wounded shows Kennedy still unhit and amiably waving to the public.

Naturally, the *Life* magazine cover photograph of Oswald holding the rifle did not escape the scrutiny of Marcus.

"The most damning piece of evidence against Oswald in the public mind is also the most damning piece of evidence against the Commission," says Marcus. "And that's the photograph of Oswald with the rifle. The best opinions available indicate definitely that this is a phony photograph. I've interviewed forty-five photographers. Three-quarters of them were willing to state flatly that this was a phony, could not be a legitimate photograph. Nobody has been able to duplicate those shadows. I have photographs of at least a dozen people that I've taken, both A and B poses. The A pose I posed, letting the body shadow control, and in each case the nose shadow falls sharply to the right, something like that. In one case, I went down to Skid Row and got three down-and-outers and paid 'em a couple of bucks each to pose."

Whether Skid Row bums or sons of Beverly Hills housewives are doing the posing, it is most assuredly possible to duplicate the shadows in the *Life* cover photo. This fact was hammered home to Marcus during a debate between Mark Lane and Commission counsel Wesley J. Liebeler, held at UCLA on January 25, 1967. Dramatically, Liebeler unveiled an oversized photograph taken in Los Angeles several days before. The nose and body shadows approximated those in the photograph in question, even though the subject did not possess the exact features of Oswald and the picture had not been taken in the same location, Dallas, on the same day of the year.

After the debate, Marcus rushed to the stage and closely examined the re-creation. "It's a fraud," he shouted. But he had no evidence of fraud other than that the picture disagreed with his own discredited theory. . . .

## Another Forum for Controversy

Until the release of his book, Marcus had been missing from the circuit of radio and television talk shows relied upon by fellow skeptics to circulate their pet theories and, at the same time, promote their particular enterprises. . . .

Depending on the tenor of their books, the Los Angeles stops fluctuated between two syndicated television shows conducted by author Louis Lomax and comedian Mort Sahl. . . .

Sahl has made his show an open forum for Mark Lane. At the same time, in his characteristic stream-of-consciousness patter, he has revealed an abysmal ignorance not only of the facts included in the Warren Report but also in related areas of evidence. . . .

On . . . a telecast of Sahl's syndicated program the host

again sat by and condoned a series of charges made by Lane without allowing the true facts to be heard. As he had done many times previously, Lane was discussing the events in the Presidential limousine after Kennedy was struck by the first bullet.

"One bullet hit him [the President] in the back," Lane theorized. "After that happened, after the bullet had struck the President, according to Roy Kellerman, the Secret Service agent in the front seat of the car, Kellerman said the President said: 'My God, I am hit.' That's the quote. 'My God, I am hit.' After that, of course, the Commission said the bullet had hit the President in the back. How could the President have said, as Roy Kellerman testified," Lane declared, "that he heard him say in a clear, distinct New England accent: 'My God, I am hit,' if the first bullet which hit him ripped through his Adam's apple?"

## Contradictions of a Secret Service Agent

Commission counsel Melvin Eisenberg had spelled out the conflict in Kellerman's testimony in an internal memorandum written to Chief Counsel J. Lee Rankin two years before, on March 7, 1964.

"Kellerman states that he heard a shot and immediately turned around looking past Governor Connally . . . to the President," Eisenberg declared. "This statement seems to be contradictory by the photographic evidence which shows Kellerman looking forward and quite unconcerned after the President had been shot the first time. It is also belied by his failure to take any affirmative action to protect the President apart from speeding up the car which apparently did not occur until after the third shot had been fired. Another contradiction in Kellerman's testimony should be noted. In his first interview on November 22, [1963], he stated that the President said 'Get me to a hospital.' In his next interview, five days later on November 27, he stated that the President said, 'My God, I've been hit.'"

A previously unpublished memorandum written by counsel Arlen Specter on March 12, 1964, further elaborated on this conflict.

"SA [Special Agents] Sibert and O'Neill stated that they interviewed Kellerman and Greer formally on November 27, 1963, and talked to them only informally at the autopsy. SA O'Neill stated that he is certain that he had a verbatim note on Kellerman's statement that the President said 'Get me to a hospital' and also that Mrs. Kennedy said 'Oh, no.' SA O'Neill stated that he was sure those were direct quotes from Kellerman because O'Neill used quotation marks in his report which indicated that he had written those precise words in his notes, which notes have since been destroyed after the report was dictated. SA O'Neill noted that Mr. Kellerman did not repeat that language in the interview of November 27, 1963, and that in the later interview O'Neill took down what Kellerman said without leading or directing him in any way.

"I also asked the two special agents about the language in their reports that Greer glanced around and noticed that the President had evidently been hit and thereafter got on the radio and communicated with the other vehicles, stating that they 'desired to get the President to the hospital immediately.' SA O'Neill and Sibert advised that to the best of their recollection SA Greer told them just that, but they probably did not make any notes on these comments since their conversation with Greer was an informal one at the time of the autopsy and they did not have an opportunity to make extensive notes in accordance with their normal interviewing procedures."

The Specter memorandum suggests that the FBI was maintaining close surveillance on the Secret Service in the days immediately following the assassination. In fact, according to one veritable report, there was discernible suspicion between the two organizations that led, for example, to both of them being represented at the Presidential autopsy conducted at Bethesda Naval Hospital. If nothing else, this informal arrangement of checks and balances indirectly aided the formulation of unbiased research and investigation for the Commission.

## The Search for Truth Continues

If the FBI and the Secret Service were not keeping tabs on each other, there were other *ad hoc* watchdogs. The assassination had attracted the interest of Jones Harris. A legendary Manhattan socialite born of two renowned stage figures, he had made a lifelong specialty of sleuthing unsolved murders. Harris had studied and meticulously enlarged an 8-millimeter motion picture showing Kennedy's mortal wound, taken by a spectator, Orville Nix. In one of the Nix frames he sighted an object behind the wall on the grassy knoll. He had enlargements made of the critical area. It then became even more apparent to Harris that he could see a station wagon on the grassy knoll. And on the roof of the vehicle he discerned a figure aiming what seemed to be a rifle.

Harris journeyed to Dallas to investigate first hand. He talked to Nix and to Abraham Zapruder. He even interviewed Zapruder's secretaries. His big find was a big fizzle. This was proven by other candid color pictures taken by another spectator. From this position, at a different angle and at a slightly higher elevation, the Harris murder car turned out to be nothing more than a space between a clump of trees.

It was Harris who was the catalyst in helping arrange the publication of various books concerning the assassination. Showing no favorites, he first introduced Josiah Thompson, Edward J. Epstein, Sylvia Meagher and Wesley J. Liebeler to interested editors.

As a result of these selfless endeavors, Harris has gained recognition as the unofficial arbiter among the in-group of superbuffs. Early in 1967 one of the superbuffs heard a rumor that an employee at Parkland Memorial Hospital in Dallas three years before had scooped up the fragments of a bullet for a souvenir. Within forty-eight hours the rumor circulated across the country from Madison Avenue in Manhattan to Harvard Street in Cambridge to Westwood Boulevard in Los Angeles to Connecticut Avenue in Washington and then back to its Manhattan source. The superbuffs had a field day. But by the time the rumor expired, not only had they failed to locate the pieces of bullet but also they could not even pinpoint the story's source.

## A New Suspect

Some of the superbuffs were even more tenacious in pursuing Igor Vaganov, an American citizen who they are convinced was part of the Dallas conspiracy. On November 7, 1963, Vaganov checked into 815 Sunset Street, Oak Cliff, Dallas, located within walking distance of the spot where officer J.D. Tippit was eventually killed. He bore a slight resemblance to Lee Harvey Oswald, although he was over six feet tall. His baggage included a 38-caliber pistol and a 250–3000 rifle with telescopic sight.

On November 21, 1963, his wife phoned her sister and informed her that Vaganov intended to do something dreadful the next day and that she was terrified.

On November 22, 1963, just after the assassination, the sister, recalling the conversation the previous day, alerted the FBI, and within hours agents traced Vaganov to his Oak Cliff apartment. He was one of twenty-eight suspects inter-rogated during a six-hour period. Vaganov offered conclu-sive support for his whereabouts at the time of the assassi-nation. The FBI eliminated him as a suspect.

Days later the agitated Vaganov notified a Philadelphia auto dealer (Vaganov had resided near Philadelphia) that he could no longer meet the time payments on his car. Several months later the dealer told the story to superbuff Vincent Salandria, who tried to track down Vaganov. Another critic, hearing the story from Salandria, contacted Gaeton J. Fonzi, an editor of *Greater Philadelphia Magazine*. Fonzi fi-nally located Vaganov through his second wife and pub-lished an article about him. After questioning Vaganov, sev-eral superbuffs decided that he lacked an airtight alibi for the time of the Tippit shooting. Suddenly, at least in their minds, he loomed strongly as a possible second assassin.

Vaganov, who seemed to be enjoying his unexpected el-evation into the limelight, next was honored at a cocktail party and paid a substantial sum of money by *Esquire* mag-azine to make a return visit to Dallas while a photographer eagerly snapped away. Vaganov posed on the site where Os-wald allegedly fired at Tippit and also in the area where it was determined that Oswald dropped his coat while fleeing from the scene of that crime.

A representative of *Esquire* introduced him to Domingo Benavides, one of the witnesses to the Tippit killing. The plot thickened as Benavides admitted he thought he recog-nized Vaganov.

What armchair detectives like the superbuffs failed to consider is that after reading the FBI reports on Vaganov and evaluating all the corroborative evidence, there can be no doubt that Vaganov is completely innocent of any com-plicity in the murder of either the President or Officer Tip-pit. Yet the superbuffs' obsession with a possible second as-sassin has compelled them to pursue this innocent man, whose wife now considers her life in danger.

The question remains who will be the next second as-sassin whose privacy will be invaded by critics with nothing else left to investigate.

# For Further Research

## Books

Michael Benson, *Who's Who in the JFK Assassination?* New York: Carol, 1993.

Jim Bishop, *The Day Kennedy Was Shot.* New York: Funk & Wagnalls, 1968.

G. Robert Blakey and Richard Billings, *The Plot to Kill the President: Organized Crime Assassinated JFK.* New York: Times Books, 1981.

Bob Callahan, *Who Shot JFK? A Guide to the Major Conspiracy Theories.* New York: Simon & Schuster, 1993.

*Dallas Morning News, November 22—The Day Remembered.* Dallas: Taylor, 1990.

Jay David, *The Weight of the Evidence: The Warren Commission and Its Critics.* New York: Meredith Press, 1968.

Edward Jay Epstein, *The Assassination Chronicles: Inquest, Counterplot, and Legend.* New York: Carroll & Graf, 1992.

James H. Fetzer, *Murder in Dealey Plaza: What We Know Now That We Didn't Know Then About the Death of JFK.* Chicago: Catfeet Press, 2000.

Jim Garrison, *A Heritage of Stone.* New York: Putnam, 1970.

——, *On the Trail of the Assassins: My Investigation and Prosecution of the Murder of President Kennedy.* New York: Sheridan Square Press, 1992.

Robert J. Groden, *The Killing of a President.* New York: Penguin, 1993.

Mark Lane, *A Citizen's Dissent: Mark Lane Replies.* New York: Holt, Rinehart, and Winston, 1968.

David S. Lifton, *Best Evidence: Disguise and Deception in the Assassination of John F. Kennedy.* New York: Macmillian, 1980.

Harrison Edward Livingstone and Robert J. Groden, *High Treason: The Assassination of JFK and the Case for Conspiracy.* New York: Carroll & Graf, 1998.

Raymond Marcus, *The Bastard Bullet: A Search for Legitimacy for Commission Exhibit 399*. Los Angeles: Raymond Marcus, 1990.

Sylvia Meagher, *Subject Index to the Warren Report and Hearings and Exhibits*. New York: Scarecrow Press, 1966.

Armand Moss, *Disinformation, Misinformation, and the "Conspiracy" to Kill JFK Exposed*. Hamden, CT: Archon Books, 1987.

Carl Oglesby, *Who Killed JFK?* Berkeley, CA: Odonian Press, 1992.

Gerald Posner, *Case Closed: Lee Harvey Oswald and the Assassination of JFK*. New York: Random House, 1993.

L. Fletcher Prouty, *JFK: The CIA, Vietnam, and the Plot to Assassinate John F. Kennedy*. New York: Carol, 1992.

David E. Scheim, *Contract on America: The Mafia Murder of President John F. Kennedy*. New York: Shapolsky, 1988.

Peter Dale Scott, *Deep Politics and the Death of JFK*. Berkeley and Los Angeles: Univeristy of California Press, 1993.

John Hanbury Angus Sparrow, *After the Assassination: A Positive Appraisal of the Warren Report*. New York: Chilmark Press, 1967.

Anthony Summers, *Conspiracy*. New York: McGraw-Hill, 1980.

Harold Weisberg, *Whitewash—The Report on the Warren Report*. New York: Dell, 1966.

## Periodicals

Luis W. Alvarez, "A Physicist Examines the Kennedy Assassination Film," *American Journal of Physics*, vol. 44 (9), 1976.

John Armstrong, "Harvey and Lee: The Case for Two Oswalds," *Probe Magazine*, July 1996; September 1997; November 1997.

Carl Bernstein, "The CIA and the Media," *Rolling Stone*, October 20, 1977.

Fred Cook, "Some Unanswered Questions," *Nation*, June 13, 1966.

Edward Jay Epstein, "Who's Afraid of the Warren Report?" *Esquire*, December 1966.

Gaeton Fonzi, "The Warren Commission, the Truth and Arlen Specter," *Greater Philadelphia Magazine*, August 1966.

Leo Sauvage, "John F. Kennedy: A Way with the People," *Time*, January 5, 1962.

———, "The Oswald Affair," *Commentary*, March 1964.

## Websites

Dealey Plaza Revisited, www.texasmonthly.com. This site revisits the day of the assassination including a cast of characters, photographs, and a time line.

JFK Assassination Research Materials, www.jfk-info.com. This site is an excellent source for JFK assassination research materials. The site includes current developments surrounding the assassination, information on the Zapruder film, Dealey Plaza photos, recommended books on JFK, and interesting links.

The Lee Harvey Oswald Research Page, www.madbbs.com. This site provides information for researchers about Lee Harvey Oswald, the accused assassin of President John F. Kennedy, as well as general assassination-related material.

NARA/JFK Assassination Records Collection/Records of the Warren Commission, www.archives.gov. The National Archives and Records Administration site provides access to the JFK assassination records including the Warren Report, information from the Assassination Records Review Board, and a JFK database for further research.

Resources for JFK Researchers, www.jfkresearch.com. For the serious JFK researcher—this site includes featured articles, related links, and a message forum.

# Index